KETO FAT BOMBS COOKBOOK

Keto Fat Bombs Recipes for Effective Fat Burning

(Easy and Exciting Low-carb Ketogenic Diet Fat Bombs for Weight Loss)

Erna Anderson

Published by Sharon Lohan

© **Erna Anderson**

All Rights Reserved

Keto Fat Bombs Cookbook: Keto Fat Bombs Recipes for Effective Fat Burning (Easy and Exciting Low-carb Ketogenic Diet Fat Bombs for Weight Loss)

ISBN 978-1-990334-19-1

All rights reserved. No part of this guide may be reproduced in any form without permission in writing from the publisher except in the case of brief quotations embodied in critical articles or reviews.

Legal & Disclaimer

The information contained in this book is not designed to replace or take the place of any form of medicine or professional medical advice. The information in this book has been provided for educational and entertainment purposes only.

The information contained in this book has been compiled from sources deemed reliable, and it is accurate to the best of the Author's knowledge; however, the Author cannot guarantee its accuracy and validity and cannot be held liable for any errors or omissions. Changes are periodically made to this book. You must consult your doctor or get professional medical advice before using any of the suggested remedies, techniques, or information in this book.

Table of contents

Part 1 1
Introduction 2
CHAPTER 1: HISTORY OF KETOGENIC DIET 4
CHAPTER 2: Hormones And The Ketogenic Diet 6
CHAPTER 3: Signs That You Are In Ketosis 13
CHAPTER 4: All About Fat 17
CHAPTER 5: IMPACTS OF THE KETOGENIC DIET 26
CHAPTER 6: When the Ketogenic Diet Should Not Be Used .. 35
CHAPTER 7: Troubleshooting Constipation 41
Keto Fat Bombs 51
Vanilla Cheesecake Fat Bombs (Serves 18) 53
Red Velvet Fat Bombs (Serves 24) 54
Vanilla Strawberry Fudge Fat Bombs (Serves 32) 56
Pina Colada Fat Bombs (Serves 16) 58
Lemon & Poppyseed Fat Bombs (Serves 18) 60
Chocolate Kisses Fat Bombs (Serves 24) 61
Pizza Fat Bombs (Serves 6) 64
Salmon Fat Bombs (Serves 6) 66
Salmon Breakfast Bombs (Serves 2) 68
Salmon and Dill Fat Bombs (Serves 12) 72
Bacon Guacamole Deviled Eggs (Serves 6) 73
Bacon Wrapped Mozzarella Sticks (Serves 2) 75
Bacon & Guacamole Fat Bombs (Serves 6) 77
Bacon, Pistachio, and Braunshweiger Truffles (Serves 12) ... 79
Egg & Bacon Fat Bombs (Serves 6) 81

Buffalo Chicken Deviled Eggs (Serves 6) 83
Bacon-Wrapped Mini Meatloaves (Serves 4) 85
Jalapeno Popper Deviled Eggs w/ Bacon 87
Cheesy Jalapeno Fat Bombs (Serves 6) 89
Savory Mediterranean Fat Bombs (Serves 5) 91
Keto Butter Burgers Fat Bombs (Serves 12) 93
Savory Sesame Fat Bombs (Serves 4) 95
Sausage Balls Fat Bombs (Serves 23) 97
Bacon Burger Bombs (Serves 12) 99
Sausage Ball Puffs (Serves 36) 101
Cheesy Bacon Fat Bombs (Serves 20) 103
Sausage & Cream Cheese Fat Bombs (Serves 8) 105
Breakfast Bacon Fat Bombs (Serves 6) 107
Baked Brie & Pecan Prosciutto Fat Bombs (Serves 1) 109
Pepperoni Pizza Fat Bombs (Serves 6) 111
Bacon Wrapped Chicken Bombs (Serves 6) 113
Conclusion 115
Part 2 117
Introduction 118
Sweet Fat Bombs 132
Vanilla Turmeric Anti-Inflammatory Keto Fat Bombs 132
Instructions: 133
Strawberry Fat Bombs 133
Ingredients: 133
Instructions: 134
Lemon Coconut Energy Balls 135
Lemon Bar Fat Bombs 136

Fudge Fat Bombs	137
Strawbwrries & Cream Fat Bombs	139
PBJ Fat Bombs	140
Pumpkin Spice Fat Bombs	142
Berries& Cream Fat Bombs	144
Dark Chocolate Peppermint Patty Fat Bombs	147
Chocolate Chip Cookie Dough Fat Bombs	149
Cinnamon Roll Fat Bombs	151
Chocolate Chip Almond Butter Fat Bombs Bars	152
French Toast Fat Bombs	154
Sea Salt Dark Chocolate Almond Cluster Fat Bombs	155
4-Ingredient Keto Coconut Fat Bombs	157
Ginger Fat Bombs	158
Keto Fat Bomb Pumpkin Pie Patties	159
Blackberry Coconut Fat Bombs	161
Caramel Apple Pie Fat Bomb	162
Coconut Oil Fat Bombs	163
Creamy Coconut and Cinnamon Fat Bombs	165
Easy Vanilla Fat Bombs	166
Craving Buster Fat Bombs	168
Single Serving Fast Method:	169
Coconut Fat Bombs	169
Peppermint Chocolate Fat Bombs	172
Raspberry Almond Chocolate Fat Bombs	173
Keto Fat Bombs with Cacao and Cashew	175
Chocolate Almond Butter Collagen Fat Bombs	177
Coconut Berry Fat Bombs	179

Samoa Fudge Bombs 180

Keto Matcha Coconut Fat Balls 183

Almond Pistachio Fat Bombs 185

Almond Butter Maple Collagen Fat Bombs 187

Coconut Carrot and Ginger Fat Bombs 189

Nutty Coconut Fat Bombs .... **Error! Bookmark not defined.**

Savoty Fat Bombs .... **Error! Bookmark not defined.**

Bacon & Egg Fat Bombs .... **Error! Bookmark not defined.**

Bacon & Guacamole Fat Bombs .... **Error! Bookmark not defined.**

Breakfast Bacon Fat Bombs .... **Error! Bookmark not defined.**

Part 1

Introduction

Introduction To The Ketogenic Diet

Ketogenic diet is one of the most popular diet that forces the body to burn fats more effectively. Many readers may not be well known with the ketogenic diet. If you are looking for the jumpstart of your fitness and health goals this diet is probably best for you. This book discuss some general ideas about ketogenic diets, as well as defining terms that may be helpful. Here you'll find an in-depth explanation about this ketogenic diet.

Many people have already experience the proven benefits for weight loss. In the most general terms, a ketogenic diet is any diet that causes ketone bodies to beproduced by the liver, shifting the body's metabolism away from glucoseand towards fat utilization. More specifically, a ketogenic eat less carbs is one that restricts carbohydrates below a certain level (generally 100 grams per day), inducing a series of adaptations to take place. Protein and fat intake are variable, depending on the goal of the dieter. However, the ultimate determinant of whether a diet is ketogenic or not is the presence (or absence) of sugars.

Fuel Metabolism And The Ketogenic Diet

Under 'normal' dietary conditions, the body runson a mix of carbohydrates, protein and fat. When carbohydrates are removed from the consume less calories, the body's small stores are quickly depleted. Consequently, the body is forced to find an alternative fuel to provide vitality.One of these fuels is free fatty acids (FFA), which can be used by most tissues in the body.However, not all organs can use FFA. For example, the brain and nervous system are unable to utilize FFA for fuel, however, they can use ketone bodies.

Ketone bodies are a by product of the incomplete breakdown of FFA in the liver.They serve as a non starch, fat derived fuel for tissues such as the brain. When ketone bodies are delivered at accelerated rates, they accumulate in the bloodstream, causing a metabolic state called ketosis to create. Simultaneously, there is a decrease in glucose utilization and production. Along with this, there is an abatement in the breakdown of protein to be used for energy, referred toas 'protein sparing'. Many individuals are drawn to ketogenic diets in a attempt to lose body fat while sparing the loss of lean body mass.

In the next chapter we discuss about the history of Ketogenic diet how it become so popular from treatment of epilepsy in the early 1900's, particularly 1920's- 1930's that was abandoned and later on was used for fasting and health restoration. The hormones, health and fitness, how our body obtains energy. What is ketosis and the creation of ketosis in our body.

CHAPTER 1: HISTORY OF KETOGENIC DIET

This chapter we will discuss the history of keto diet, as during 1990s, fat was demonized. The macronutrient became the dirty word of the nutrition industry, and was shunned by consumers and professionals a like. Many believed that fat was the essential cause of a host of health problems, including weight gain, high cholesterol, and heart disease, although there was no any sufficient scientific evidence to support these claims. Despite what the science showed, however, people began jumping on the low fat band wagon, turning to low fat alternatives that were loaded with sugar and carbohydrates instead. As more fat free and low fat products became available, the average American became bigger. By 2001, about one third of the American population was over weight. The prevalence of heart disease increased and diabetes rates soared. So what went wrong.

Crisp whole foods such as meat, eggs, cream, and butter, the foods your ancestors ate for centuries were being replaced with low fat Franken foods such as margarine, low fat snack cookies, and skim milk. These foods were not only full of sugar and carbohydrates, some were also loaded with artificial ingredients. When these substances are consumed regularly, over time, the human body reacts by gaining weight, showing symptoms of fatigue and brain fog, and succumbing to chronic conditions. Although scientific research produced findings to the contrary, fat especially saturated fat had developed a lasting reputation for being awful for you. Although the low fat diet craze eventually dwindled, the damage was done fat was shunned.

Now this may stun you after all, it is likely that you have been told for years or even decades to eat plenty of whole grain carbohydrates and avoid saturated fat like the plague yet fat is good for you. Fat even perhaps specially, saturated fat, helps your body run like a well oiled machine. Your body's need for fat is the basis of the ketogenic diet, which encourages that you get most of your calories around 75 percent from fat and only 5 to 10 percent from carbohydrates. The remaining calories come from high quality proteins.

The ketogenic diet is not a new trend or a fad diet. It is actually been around for decades. It was used in the 1920s as the main treatment method for difficult to control epilepsyin young children and it worked remarkably well. Eventually, it fell out of fashion with the increasing availability of anti seizure medications. People preferred a quick fix even if that fix meant the potential for more side effects. Today, people following nutritional ketogenic diets report weight loss, increased energy levels, better mood, improved concentration, and mental clarity. Nevertheless, standard media and even some health care professionals tend to present the ketogenic diet in a negative light. Like fat, ketones, which are mixes made when the body begins using fat instead of carbohydrates for energy, have a bad reputation. Most of the concerns encompassing ketones and the ketogenic diet are unfounded or are a result of confusion between the terms "ketosis" and " ketoacidosis." The European Journal of Clinical Nutrition states that this confusion and preconceived notions about the ketogenic diet like the idea that all fat is bad for you may be "presenting unnecessary barriers to the use as therapeutic tools in the physician 'shand."

So now let' sput the rumors to rest and understand why fat is not just great however is essential to maintaining optimal health. It is actually sugar, carbohydrates, and processed vegetable oils that are largely responsible for weight gain and the increasing rates of chronic health conditions. Limiting carbohydrates and replacing them with both immersed and unsaturated fats the basis of the ketogenic diet can not only help you lose weight, it can help you stay healthy for years to come.

CHAPTER 2: Hormones And The Ketogenic Diet

Ketogenic diets cause the adaptations described above principally by affecting the levels of two hormones: insulin and glucagon. Insulin is a storage hormone, responsible for moving nutrients out of the bloodstream and into target tissues. For case, insulin causes glucose to be stored in muscleas glycogen, and FFA to be stored in adipose tissue as triglycerides. Glucagon is a fuel mobilizing hormone, stimulating the body to break down stored glycogen, especially in the liver, to provide glucose for the body.

When carbohydrates are removed from the diet, insulin levels decrease and glucagon levels increase. This causes an increase in FFA release from fat cells, and increased FFA burning in the liver. The quickened FFA burning in the liver is what ultimately leads to the production of ketone bodies and the metabolic state of ketosis. In addition to insulin and glucagon, a number of other hormones are also affected, all of which help to shift fuel use away from carbohydrates and towards fat.

Exercise And The Ketogenic Diet

As with any fat loss diet, exercise will improve the achievement of the ketogenic diet.However, a diet devoid of carbohydrates is unable to maintain high intensity exercise performance although low intensity exercise may be performed. For this reason, individuals who wish to use a ketogenic diet and perform high intensity exercise must integrate carbohydrates without disrupting the effects of ketosis.

Two altered ketogenic abstains from food are described in this book which approach this issue from different directions. The targeted ketogenic diet (TKD) allows carbohydrates to be expended immediately around exercise, to sustain performance without affecting ketosis. The cyclical ketogenic diet (CKD) alternates times of ketogenic dieting with periods of high carbohydrate utilization. The period of high carbohydrate eating refills muscle glycogen to sustain exercise performance.

What Is Ketosis
Your body's second preferred source of energy is fat, when carbohydrates are not easily accessible, your body turns to fat to get the energy it needs. When this happens, the liver breaks down fat into fatty acids and then breaks down these fatty acids into an energy rich substance called ketones or ketone bodies. The presence of ketone bodies in the blood is called ketosis. The goal of a ketogenic diet is to kick your body into long term ketosis, essentially turning it into a fat burning machine.

How Your Body Obtains Energy
Your cells need a constant supplyof energy to stay alive and keep you alive. Even when you are sitting on the couch doing nothing, your body is generating energy for your cells. Since energy can not be created, only converted from one form to another, your body needs to get this energy from somewhere, soit uses the food you eat. Your body can use each macro nutrient carbohydrates, fat, and protein for energy. The biochemical process of obtaining energy is a complicated one, but it is simportant to understand the basics so you can get a feel for how ketosis works on a cellular level.

Energy From Protein
Protein is the body's least favorite macronutrient to use as energy. This is because protein serves so many other functions in the body, way more than any other macronutrient. Protein provides structural support to every cell in your body and helps maintain your body tissues. Proteins act as enzymes that play a

role in all of the chemical reactions in your body. Without these enzymes, these chemical reactions would be so slow that your body would not be able to carry out basic processes like digestion and metabolism and you would not be able to survive. Proteins also help maintain fluid and acid base balance, help transport substances such as oxygen through the body and waste out of the body, and act as anti bodies to keepyour immune system strong and help fight off illness.

This process of using protein for energy is what makes extreme calorie restriction dangerous. When your diet does not provide enough calories, your body begins to break down the protein in your muscles for energy, which can lead to muscle loss or muscle wasting in addition to nutritional deficiencies.

Proteins are made up of amino acids. When you eat proteins, your body breaks them down into their individual amino acids, which are then converted into sugars through a process called deamination. Your body can use these protein turned sugars as a form of energy, but that means your body is not using the amino acids for those other important functions. It is best to avoid forcing the body to use protein for energy, and you do that by providing it with the other nutrients it needs. That being said, if the body has no other choice but to use protein for energy, it will.

Energy From Carbohydrates

Although your body is adept at using any food that is available for energy, it always turns to carbohydrates first. When you eat carbohydrates, they are broken down into glucose or another sugar that is easily converted to glucose. Glucose is absorbed through the walls of the small intestine and then enters your body by way of your blood stream, which causes your blood glucose levels to rise. As soon as the glucose enters your blood, your pancreas sends out insulin to pick up the sugar and carry it to your cells so they can use it as energy.

Once your cells have used all the glucose they need at that time, much of the remaining glucose is converted into glycogen (the storage form of glucose), which is then stored in the liver and muscles. The liver has a limited ability to store glycogen, though, it can only store enough glycogen to provide you with energy for about 24 hours. All the extra glucose that can not be stored is converted into triglycerides, the storage form of fat, and stored in your fat cells.

This process of using protein for energy is what makes extreme calorie restriction dangerous. When your diet does not provide enough calories, your body begins to break down the protein in your muscles for energy, which can lead to muscle loss or muscle wasting in addition to nutritional deficiencies.

When you do not eat for a few hours and your blood sugar starts to drop, your body will call on the glycogen stored in the liver and muscles for energy before anything else. The pancreas releases a hormone called glucagon, which triggers the release of glucose from the glycogen stored in your liver to help raise your blood sugar levels. This process is called glycogenolysis. The glycogen stored in your liver is used exclusively to in crease your blood glucose levels, while the glycogen stored in your muscles is used strictly as fuel for your muscles. When you eat carbohydrates again, your body uses the glucose it gets from them to replenish those glycogen stores. If you regularly eat carbohydrates, your body never has a problem getting access to glucose for energy and the stored fat stays where it is in your fat cells.

Energy From Fat

The body prefers to use carbohydrates for energy because they are easily accessible and fast acting, but in the absence of carbohydrates, your body turns to fat. The fat from the food you eat is broken down into fatty acids, which enter the blood stream through the walls of the small intestine. Most of your cells can directly use fatty acids for energy, but some specialized cells, such as the cells in your brain and your muscles, can not run on fatty acids directly. To appease these cells and give them the energy they need, your body uses fatty acids to make ketones.

The Creation Of Ketones

When your body does not have access to glucose for example, during times of fasting or when intentionally following a low carbohydrate diet it turns to fat for energy. Fat is taken to the liver where it is broken down into glycerol and fatty acids through a process called beta oxidation. The fatty acid molecules are further broken down through a process called ketogenesis, and a specific ketone body called acetoacetate is formed.

Over time, as your body becomes adapted to using ketones as fuel, your muscles convert acetoacetate into beta hydroxybutyrate or BHB, which is the preferred ketogenic source of energy for your brain, and acetone, most of which is expelled from the body as waste.

The glycerol created during beta oxidation goes through a process called gluconeogenesis. During gluconeogenesis, the body converts glycerol into glucose that your body can use for energy.Your body can also convert excess protein into glucose. Your body does need some glucose to function, but it does not need carbohydrates to get it. It does a good job of converting whatever it can into the simple sugar.

Ketosis And Weight Loss

Now that you understand how your body creates energy and how ketones are formed, you may be left pondering how this translates into weight loss. When you eat a considerable measure of carbohydrates, your body happily burns them for vitality and stores any excessas glycogen in your liver or as triglycerides in your fat cells. When you take carbohydrates out of the e?uation, your body depletesits glycogen stores in the liver and muscles and then turns to fat for energy. Your body obtains energy from the fat in the food you eat, however it also uses the triglycerides, or fats, stored in your fat cells. When your body starts burning put away fat, your fat cells shrink and you begin to lose weight and become leaner.

How To Induce Ketosis
Inducing ketosis not an easy task, yet once you get the hang of it, it can become second nature. The first step in actuating ketosis verely to limit carbohydrate consumption, however that is not enough.You must limit your protein consumption as well. Traditional low carbohydrate diets do not induce ketosis because they allow a high in take of protein.

Because your body is able to convert excess protein into glucose, your body never switches over to burning fat as fuel. You can induce ketosis by following a highfat diet that allows moderate amounts of protein and allows only a small amount of carbohydrates or what is called a ketogenic diet.

The exact percentage of each macronutrient you need to kick your body into ketosis may vary from person toperson, yet in general, the macronutrient ratio falls into the following ranges:

60 – 75 percent of calories from fat
15 – 30 percent of calories from protein
5– 10 percent of calories from carbohydrates

This largely differs from both a standard low carbohydrate diet, which typically allows more calories to come from protein, and the traditional dietary reference in takes set by the Institute of Medicine.

Currently, the Institute of Medicine recommends getting 45 – 65 percent of your calories from carbohydrates, 20 – 35 percent of your calories from fat, and 10 – 35 percent of your calories from protein. Although the individual recommendations of low carbohydrate diets differ based on which one you follow, they typically allow about 20 percent of calories from carbohydrates, 25 – 30 percent from protein, and 55 – 65 percent fromfat.

Once you are in ketosis, you have to continue with the high fat, low carbohydrate, moderate protein plan. Eating too numerous carbohydrates or too much protein can kick you out of ketosisat any time by providing your body with enough glucose to stop using fat as fuel.

CHAPTER 3: Signs That You Are In Ketosis

Signs that you are in ketosis may begin appearing after only one week of following a true ketogenic diet. For a few people, it can take longer as much as three months. The amount of time it takes for you to start seeing signs that your bodyis burning fat for fuel largely depends on you as an individual. When signs do begin to appear, they are pretty similar crosswise over the board.

Keto "Influenza"
"Keto influenza" or "low carb influenza" commonly affects people in the first few days of starting a ketogenic diet. Obviously, the ketogenic diet does not actually cause seasonal influenza, how ever the phenomenon is given the term because it is symptoms closely resemble that of the flu. It would be more accurate to refer to this stage as a carbohydrate withdrawal, because that is really what it is.When you take carbohydrates away, it causes altered hormonal states and electrolyte imbalances that are responsible for the associated symptoms. The basic symptoms include headache, nausea, upset stomach, sleepiness, fatigue, abdominal cramps, diarrhea, and lack of mental clarity, or what is commonly referred to as "brain fog."
Carbohydrate addiction is a real thing. Some research shows that carbohydrates activate certain stimuli in the brain that can be reliance forming and cause addiction. Carbohydrate addicts have wild cravings for carbohydrates, and when they do eat them, they tend to orgy. In a carbohydrate addict, the removal of starches can cause withdrawal side effects, such as dizziness and irritability, and intense cravings.
The duration of symptoms varies it depends on you as an individual, yet typically a "keto influenza" endures anywhere from a couple of days to a week. In uncommon cases, it can last

up to two weeks. Some of the indications of the "keto influenza" are associated with dehydration, because in the starting stages of ketosis you lose a lot of water weight. With that lost fluid, you also lose electrolytes. You can renew these electrolytes by drinking enhanced waters (however make sure they are not sweetened) and drinking lots of home made bone broth. This may help lessen the severity of the symptoms.

Bad Breath
Unfortunately, bad breath is another early sign that you are in ketosis. When you are in ketosis, your body makes $CH_3)2CO$ as a waste product. Some of this acetone is released in your breath, giving it a fruity or ammonia like quality. You can combat bad breath by chewing on fresh mint leaves and drinking plenty of water, since bad breath is also associated with dehydration.

Decreased Appetite and Nausea
As your body adapts to a ketogenic slim down, you may have a decreased appetite. This is because you are giving your body with plenty of fat and protein, which are both highly satiating, and not a great deal of carbohydrates. The nausea associated with "keto influenza" can also decrease your appetite.When you reach this stage, it is important that you eat even if you feel like you are not hungry. You want to make sure your body is getting enough calories and supplements, especially in this time of transition.

Increased Energy
When the fog starts to clear and your body starts to become keto adapted, the uncomfortable symptoms you were feeling will dissipate and you will begin tosee the benefits of following a ketogenic diet. One of the first beneficial signs many people experience is an increment in energy. When your body breaks down fat instead of carbohydrates, more energy is produced gram for gram, leaving you feeling alert and energized.

Improved Focus And Mental Clarity
Many mental issues, such as brain fog and problems with memory, are caused by what is called neurotoxicity, the exposure of the nervous system to toxic substances. For the brain, exposure to too much glucose can result in neurotoxicity. When you reduce the supply of glucose in your body and your brain starts to use ketonesas fuel, the toxicity levels diminish. As a result, you may be able to think more clearly, focus better, and have better memory recall.

Other Possible Signs Of Ketosis Include:
- Cold hands and feet Increased urinary frequency Difficulty sleeping
- Metallic taste in the mouth Dry mouth
- Increased thirst
- Measurable Ketones

Your body is pretty good at letting you know when you are in ketosis without any testing, but if you want to be absolutely sure, you can test your ketone levels with urine strips or a blood meter. Urine strips allow you to easily test for the presence of ketones in your urine, while blood meter scan test for ketones with a small blood sample from a prick in your finger. These testing methods tend to be more reliable than just trusting the presence of symptoms, and if you really want to know ifyou are producing ketones, they are a great way to find out, but sometimes they can be in accurate.

Although these signs are common among many people who follow a ketogenic diet, your experience may be different. Every body is uni?ue, so it is impossible to say exactly what your personal experience will be. Keep in mind that in the early stages of ketosis, your symptoms may be unpleasant, but as your body adapts, you will begin to experience the benefits of following a ketogenic diet plan.

Carbohydrate addiction is a real thing. Some research shows that carbohydrates activate certain stimuli in the brain that can be dependence forming and cause addiction. Carbohydrate addicts have uncontrollable cravings for carbohydrates, and when they do eat them, they tend to binge. In a carbohydrate addict, the removal of carbohydrates can cause withdrawal symptoms, such as dizziness and irritability, and intense cravings.

CHAPTER 4: All About Fat

If you are one of the people who followed a low fat diet and failed to lose weight, or failed to see any other major health improvements, do not worry, you are in the company of millions. When the popularity of the low fat diet surged, many followers found themselves gaining more weight. Removing fat from your diet was supposed to make you thinner and healthier, but it did just the opposite. When people started replacing fats with carbohydrates and low fat alternatives, the incidences of diabetes and obesity began to sky rocket. Could the beloved low fat diet be to blame? Absolutely.

Low Fat Diet Myths
If you are still on the low fat diet train, read this next sentencec are fully and really let it sink in: Fat is not your enemy, sugar is. And that applies to all forms of sugar, not only the granulated stuff that you put in your coffee in the morning. Sure, the sugar in fruit is packaged with vitamin C, potassium, fiber, and other valuable nutrients, which makes it a far superior choiceover regular old sugar, but overdoing it can actually hinder weight loss efforts and set you up for other health problems. But before delving too deeply into sugar, it is important to spend some time debunking the myths that have surrounded the word "fat" for years.
As the low fat diet began to gain popularity, there was also an increase in the availability of low fat food items, such as cookies and candy bars. To create these items, manufacturers removed fat and replaced it with sugar to keep it palatable so consumers would continue to buy the product. These packaged food items were lower in fat, but they were higher in sugar and contained the same, if not more, calories.

Eating Fat Makes You Fat

On the surface, the theory that eating fat makes you fat seems like a no brainer. Of the three macronutrients protein, carbohydrates, and fat, fat contains the most calories per gram. Protein and carbohydrates have 4 calories per gram, while fat contains more than twice that at 9 calories per gram. It would make sense that if you cut out fat or replace fat with protein or carbohydrates at each meal, you would be saving yourself at on of calories throughout the course of the day. While technically you would save on calories, it does not lead to sustainable weight loss.

In order to understand why fat does not make you fat, you have to understand how you gain weight in the first place. The simple explanation is this: You start thinking about food and your body secretes insulin in response. The insulin triggers a response that tells your body to store fatty acids instead of using them for energy, so you get hungry. When you get hungry, you eat. If you are on a low fat diet, your lunch may consist of two slices of whole wheat toast with a couple of slices of turkey no cheese, no mayo and an apple on the side. If you have subscribed to the low fat diet theory, this seems like a healthy meal, but in reality, it is loaded with carbohydrates that pass through your digestive system quickly, causing significant spikes in blood sugar, and has virtually no fat.

Carbohydrates are a fast acting source of energy for your body, but they do not do a lot to fill you up. Even carbohydrates that are loaded with fiber are far less satisfying than either protein or fat. If you want your meal to be truly satisfying, make sure it contains plenty of fat.

Your body quickly breaks down your high carbohydrate meal, which sends a rush of glucose into your blood stream. Your body responds to this glucose by secreting more insulin, which carries the glucose out of your blood and into your cells. Once the glucose levels drop, you get hungry again, your body secretes more insulin, and the cyclestarts over.

Now here is where you will want to pay close attention. Your body is main regulator of fat metabolism is insulin. Insulin controls lipo protein lipase, or LPL, an enzyme that pulls fat into your cells. The higher your insulin levels, the more fat LPL pullsin to your cells. Translation: when insulin levels increase, you store fat. When insulin levels drop, you burn fat for energy. The main thing that affects insulin levels is carbohydrates, not fat. So when you eat a lot of carbohydrates, your insulin levels increase, which increases your LPL levels, which increases your storage of fat.

It is important to remember that over doing it on any of the nutrients will lead to weight gain. Regularly exceeding your calorie needs will cause weight gain regard less of whether you do it with carbohydrates, protein, or fat, but fat is not the major culprit when it comes to weight gain.

Cholesterol Causes Heart Disease

The cholesterol you eat actually has very little impact on your blood cholesterol levels for two reasons. The first reason is that your body does not absorb dietary cholesterol very efficiently. Most of the cholesterol you eat goes right through your digestive tract and never even enters your blood stream. The second reason is that the amount of cholesterol in your blood is tightly controlled by your body. When you eat a lot of dietary cholesterol, your body shuts down its own production of cholesterol to compensate. There is a percentage of the populace, however, that is hypersensitive to dietary cholesterol. For these people about 25 percent of the population dietary cholesterol does cause modest increases in both LDL (low density lipo protein) and HDL (high thickness lipo protein) levels, however even so, the increased cholesterol levels do not increase the risk of heart disease. In fact, both the Framing ham Heart Study and the Honolulu Heart Program Study both found the opposite to be true: low cholesterol levels were actually associated with increased risk of death. A separate study published in the Journal of the American Medical Association reported findings that neither high LDL ("bad" cholesterol) levels nor low HDL ("good" cholesterol) levels were important risk factors for death from coronaryartery disease or heart attack.

Most of the cholesterol in your blood (75 percent) is actually made in your body. Only 25 percent comes from the food you eat. On the off chance that you followed a completely cholesterol free diet, your body would compensate by increasing it is cholesterol production by the liver to keep your blood levels steady. That is because your body needs cholesterol to survive.

Cholesterol is absolutely essential for your survival. This lipo protein, as it is physiologically classified, performs three major functions. It makes up the bile acids that help you digest food, it allows the body to make vitamin D and other essential hormones such asestrogen and testosterone, and it is a component of the outer coating of everyone of your cells. Without cholesterol, your body would literally crumble.

Now that is not to say that you should throw all caution out the window when it comes to cholesterol, yet you need to pay attention to the right thing, and that is the size of the cholesterol particles in your blood stream rather than the total numbers. Cholesterol comes in two forms: large particles that "bounce" off the arterial wall sand small, dense particles that stick to the walls of your arteries and contribute to arterial blockage, which can eventually lead to heart disease. The problem is that so much focus is placed on the total numbers that many people fail to pay attention to cholesterol particle size.

According to research, it is not fat that causes the accumulation of small, densecholesterol particles in your blood, it is sugar. Also, that is sugar in any form, including refined carbohydrates. Sugar decreases the amount of the large cholesterol particles in your blood, creates the small damaging cholesterol particles, increases triglyceride levels, and contributes to prediabetes.

Saturated Fat Causes Heart Disease

The other wide spread belief is that eating saturated fat causes an increase in the amount of cholesterol in your blood, which in turn causes heart disease or increases your risk of heart disease. This theory was developed from some human and animal studies that were done decades ago. However, more recent research calls these theories into question.

Why Fat Is Your Friend
Fat is an integral part of every cell in your body. This macronutrient is a major component of your cell membranes, which hold each cell together. Every single cell in your body, from the cells in your mind to the cells in your heart to the cells in your lungs, is dependent on fat for survival. Fat is especially important for your brain, which is made up of 60 percent fat and cholesterol. Fat and cholesterol are used as building blocks for many hormones, which help regulate metabolism, control growth and development, and maintain boneand muscle mass, among many other things. Fat is vital for proper immune function, helps manage body temperature, and serves as a source of protection for your major organs. Fat surrounds all of your key organs to provide a sort of cushion for protection against falls and trauma. Fatal so helps boost metabolic function and plays a role in keeping you lean.

Fat is an essential nutrient. This means that you need to ingest it through the foods you eat because the body can not make what it needs on its claim. Fat is composed of individual molecules called fatty acids. Two of these fatty acids, omega 3 fatty acids and omega 6 fatty acids, are absolutely essential for good health.Omega 3 fatty acids play a crucial role in brain function and development, while omega 6 fatty acids help regulate metabolism and maintain bone health. Fat also allows you to absorb and digest other essential nutrients, such as vitamins A, D, E, and K and beta carotene. Without enough fat in your diet, you would not be able to absorb any of these nutrients and you would eventually develop nutritional deficiencies.

As if that was not enough, fat is a major source of energy for your body. The fact that each gram of fat contains 9 caloriesis actually a good thing. This makes it a compact source of energy that your body can use easily and efficiently. Unlike with carbohydrates, which your body can just store in limited amounts, your body has an unlimited ability to store fat for later use. When food intake falls short, as between meals or while you are sleeping, your body calls on it is fat reservoirs for energy. This physiological processis what the entire ketogenic diet is based on your body needs a continuous source of energy to maintain it is functions. The body is preferred source of energy, because it is fast acting and easily accessible, is glucose, which comes from carbohydrates. When you give your body access to glucose, it stores fat in your fat cells for later use.When you deprive the body of glucose, it turns to fat for energy.

Reducing Body Fat
Now that you know what causes your body to store fat, the obvious next question is, how do you use that knowledge to help reduce your body fat? The quick answer, and one that may seem counter intuitive eat this point, is to eat more fat, however it is not that simple. You can not simply include fat to a diet that is full of carbohydrates and loaded with protein and expect the weight to fall off. You have to make a strategic plan to follow a diet that allows you to eat a significant amount of fat while also limiting carbohydrate consumption and eating a moderate amount of protein. In other words: a ketogenic diet.

The Importance of a Healthy Body Fat Level
Fat is important, there is no doubt about that, yet too much on your body can be bad for your health. Having excess body fat increases your risk of various well being problems, including:

- Certain typesof cancers
- Type 2 diabetes

- Heart disease
- Gallstones
- Osteoarthritis
- Sleepapnea
- Gestational diabetes
- Stroke
- Fatty liver disease
- Infertility
- Kidney disease
- High blood pressure

Reducing the amount of fat you carry on your body can help reduce your risk of developing these chronic conditions, even if you havea family history of them.

Improving Your Blood Sugar and Insulin Levels
A major component to keeping yourself healthy, or improving any current health problems, is regulating your blood sugar and insulin levels. Imbalances in blood sugar and insulin are significant factors in the rapidly developing epidemic in diabetes in both children and adults.

Insulin Resistance and Diabetes
You already know that insulin is responsible for bringing the glucose from your blood stream into your cells so that your body can use it as energy, how ever insulin also stimulates your liver and muscles to store excess glucose, which is called glycogen, for later use. In a healthy person, insulin and glucose do their occupations effectively and efficiently, and as a result, both insulin and glucose levels remain within a certain healthy range.

Insulin resistance is a condition in which the pancreas produces enough insulin, however the body does not use it effectively. When you are repeatedly presented to high levels of insulin, your cells begin tosay, "No, thank you" and start building up a resistance to insulin. When insulin, which carries glucose on its back, can not enter the cells, glucose remains in the blood stream as well. This signals the pancre as to release even more insulin, which only exacerbates the cycle. While your body may be able to sustain this added stress for a certain period of time, eventually the pancreas gives up and insulin production decreases or stops altogether.

Many people are not aware that they have insulin resistance until they are officially diagnosed with pre diabetes or type 2 diabetes. Early warning signs of insulin protection include fatigue, energy crashes, carbohydrate cravings, and weight gain around the mid section. On the off chance that you experience anyof these warning signs, it may be beneficial to have your insulin and glucose levels tested.

Without insulin, glucose can not enter the cells, so it stays in the blood stream, wreaking havoc on your system. This is the point when many people are diagnosed with pre diabetes or type 2 diabetes. Elevated glucose levels also contribute to weight, high blood pressure, heart disease, certain types of cancer, and neurode generative disorders such as Alzheimer's disease.

Effect Of Carbohydrate,
When you eat carbohydrates, your body breaks them down into glucose. The rate at which this happens differs depending on the type of carbohydrates you are eating, however eventually, all carbohydrates, with the exception of fiber, become glucose. When glucose enters your blood stream, it triggers the release of insulin, as you already know. Constantly bombarding your body with carbohydrates and refined sugars increases glucose and insulin levels dramatically, increasing your risk of developing insulin resistance and the other resulting health problems. The goal is to avoid surges and crashes in glucose and insulin and to keep your levels consistent and steady throughout the day. When you do this, your body is better able to handle both glucose and insulin over the long term.

How Fat Can Help
Unlike carbohydrates and refined sugars, eating fat does not cause a dramatic spike in glucose or insulin levels. When you turn your body from burning glucose for fuel to burning fat for fuel, which is the basis of the ketogenic diet, you help stabilize your glucose and insulin levels, which decreases your chances of developing insulin resistance.

Feeling Satisfied While Losing Weight
One of the biggest complaints you will hear from dieters on a weight loss program is that they do not feel satisfied. They are always hungry or the food just is not good.This is where most diets fail.In case you are always hungry on a diet, what are the chances that you are going to be able to stick to it long haul? Probably close to zero. No one wants to be hungry all the time. On the other hand, consistently eating foods that lack any season and always leave you wanting more is a recipe for disaster. At some point, your desires for delicious, satiating foods are going to triumph over your determination to lose weight and you are going to give into temptation and probably in a big way. Feelings of deprivation are one of the biggest causes of eventual binges. This is where fat shines.
Foods with a high fat content tend to taste so good because many distinctive flavors dissolve in fats. Butter especially works as a excellent carrier for a wide variety of flavors, including spices, vanilla, and other fat soluble ingredients. The human body is also genetically programmed to seek out high energy foods. Because of this, fatty foods are inherently saw as more flavorful.
Of the three macronutrients, fat is the generally satiating. Sure it is the calorie densest, too, however it helps you fill up faster and keeps you full longer, which means that you are likely to take in fewer calories over the long term and you are less prone to wild gorges.

When you cut fat out of your diet, it is hard to reach that point when you really feel satisfied. This is why peopleon low fat diets complain of being hungry all the time. Fat also adds a ton of flavor to food, so when you eat fat you are actually enjoying the food you are eating, which makes you more likely to stick to your diet plan. Sounds likea no brainer, right?

CHAPTER 5: IMPACTS OF THE KETOGENIC DIET

The ketogenic diet has numerous metabolic impacts, many of which are discussed in the previous sections. However there are numerous other metabolic impacts that need to be discussed as well as concerns which are typically raised regarding the ketogenic diet.
This section is a catch all to discuss any effects on the body that have not been discussed in past. It examines the effects (and side effects) of the metabolic state of ketosis on the human body.As well, some of the major well being concerns which have been voiced regarding the ketogenic diet are addressed here.
There are ultimately two main concerns regarding the ketogenic diet in terms of health dangers. The first is the potential negative effects of the 'high protein' intake of the ketogenic diet. Additionally, there is the effect of high levels of ketones. They are discussed as needed underneath.

Long Term Effects
There are few studies of the long term effects of a ketogenic diet. One of the few, which took after two explorers over a period of 1 year was done almost 70 years ago (1). Beyond that study, the two models most often used to examine the effects of the ketogenic diet are the Inuit and pediatric epilepsy patients. Epileptic children have been studied extensively, and are kept in ketosis for periods up to three years. In this group, the major

side effects of the ketogenic diet are elevated blood lipids, stoppage, water soluble vitamin deficiency, increased rate of kidneystones, growth inhibition, and acidosis during ailment.

However, the pediatric epilepsy diet is not identical the typical ketogenic diet used by health food nuts and healthy adults, especially in terms of protein intake, and may not provide a perfect model. While studies of epileptic children give some understanding into possible long term effectsof a ketogenic diet, it should be noted that there are no studies of the long term impacts of a CKD or similar diet approach. The consequences of alternating between a ketogenic and non ketogenic metabolism are a total unknown. For this reason, it is not recommended that a CKD, or any ketogenic diet, be followed indefinitely.

Insulin Resistance

Although low sugar diets tend to normalize insulin and blood glucose levels in many individuals, a little known effect is increased insulin resistance when carbohydrates are refed. There is little look into concerning the physiological effects of refeeding carbohydrates after long term ketogenic dieting although fasting has been studied to some degree. Early ketogenic diet writing mentions a condition called 'alloxan' or 'starvation diabetes', referring to an initial insulin resistance when carbohydrates are reintroduced to the diet following carbohydrate restriction.

In brief, the initial physiological response to carbohydrate refeeding looks similar to what is seen in Type II diabetics, namely blood sugar swings and hyperinsulinemia. This type of response is also seen in individuals on a CKD. It should be noted that this response did not occur universally in research, being more prevalent in those who had pre existing glucose control problems. Too, exercise appears to affect how well or poorly the body handles sugars during refeeding.

One hypothesis for this effect was that ketones them selves meddled with insulin restricting and glucose utilization yet this was shown not to be the case (3,4). In fact, ketones may actually improve insulin binding. The exact reason for this 'insulin resistance was not determined until much later. The change was ultimately found to becaused by changes in enzyme levels, especially in those enzymes involved in both fat and sugar burning. High levels of free greasy acid levels also affect glucose transport and use .

Long periods of time without carbohydrate utilization leads to a down regulation in the proteins responsible for carbohydrate burning. Further more, high levels of free fatty acids in the blood stream may impair glucose transport.

This change occurs both in the liver and in the muscle. During carbohydrate refeeding, the body up regulates levels of these chemicals yet there is a delay amid which the body may have trouble storing and utilizing dietary carbohydrates. This delay is approximately 5 hours to up regulate liver enzyme levels and anywhere from 24 – 48 hours in muscle tissue.While there is a decrease in sugar oxidation in the muscle, this is accompanied by an increase in glycogen storage.

These time courses for enzyme up regulation correspond well with what is often seen in individuals on a CKD, which is really nothing more than a ketogenic diet followed by carbohydrate refeeding done on a weekly basis. Frequently, individuals will report the presence of urinary ketones during the first few hours of their carb loading period, seeming to contradict the idea that carbohydrates always interrupt ketosis. This suggests that the liver is continuing to oxidize fat at an accelerated rate and that ingested starches are essentially not being 'perceived' by the liver.

After around 5 hours, when liver enzymes up regulate, urinary ketone levels commonly decreaseas liver glycogen begins to refill.Another interesting aspect of carbohydrate refeeding is that liver glycogen is not initially refilled by incoming glucose. Rather glucose is released into the circulation system for muscle glycogen resynthesis (particularly if muscle glycogen storesare depleted) initially, refilling liver glycogen later.

In practice, many individuals report what appears to be rebound hypoglycemia (low blood sugar) either amid the carb upor during the first few days of eating carbohydrates when ketogeniceating is finished, for the reasons discussed above.

Ketones them selves do not appear to alter how cells respond to insulin which goes against the popular belief that ketogenic diets by one means or another modify fat cells, making them more likely to store fat when the ketogenic consume less calories is ended. Functional experience shows this to be true, as many people have little trouble maintaining their muscle versus fat levels when the ketogenic diet is stopped, especially if their activity patterns are maintained.

Appetite Suppression

An unusual effect of complete fasting is a general diminish in hunger after a short period of time. Also, studies which restrict carbohydrate yet allow 'unlimited' fat and protein find that calorie consumption goes down thought about to normal levels further suggesting a connection between ketosis and appetite.

Since continued fasting causes an increase in ketone bodies in the blood stream, achieving a maximum in 2 – 3 weeks, it was always assumed that ketones were the cause of the appetite suppression. As with many aspects of ketosis (in this case starvation ketosis), this assumption was never directly studied and propagated itself through the literature without challenge. Recent inquire about shows that ketones per se are most likely not the cause of the decreased appetite during ketosis.

First, is the moderately higher fat content of the ketogenic diet compared too ther diets. Fat tends to moderate digestion, implying that food stays in the stomach longer, providing a sense of fullness.The same has been shown to for protein. Additionally, protein stimulates the release of the hormone cholecysto kinin (CCK) which is thought to help regulate appetite.

However, studies using very low calorie intake (and hence low dietary fat intakes) have documented this same blunting of appetite, suggesting a different mechanism. Rather than the effects of dietary fat, the researchers argue that what is perceived as a blunting of appetiteis simply an arrival to base line hunger levels.

That is, amid the introductory stages of a diet, there is an increase in appetite, which is followed by a decrease over time. It is this diminish which is being interpreted by health food nut's as a blunting of appetite.

By and large, the data supporting an appetite suppressing impact of ketogenic diets points to a mechanism other than ketones. This is not to say that craving may not be suppressed on a ketogenic diet, only that it is most likely not ketones or metabolic ketosis which are the cause of the suppression.

Anecdotally, some individuals have a solid suppression of appetite while others do not. This discrepancy can probably be ascribed to individual differences. In the event that a health food nut's hunger is stifled substantially on a ketogenic diet, it may be difficult for them to consume the necessary calories. In this case, the use of calorically dense foods such as mayonnaise and vegetable oils can be used to increase caloric in take. On the off chance that appetite is not smothered on a ketogenic diet, less calorically dense food scan be consumed.

Cholesterol levels
The relatively high fat in take of the ketogenic diet immediately raises concerns regarding the effects on blood lipids and the potential for increases in the risk for heart disease, stroke, etc. Several key players in relative risk for these diseasesare low density lipo proteins (LDL, or 'bad cholesterol'), high density lipo proteins (HDL, or 'great cholesterol') and blood triglyceride levels (TG). High levels of total cholesterol, and high levels of LDL

correlate with increased disease chance. High levels of HDL are thought to apply a protective effect against cholesterol related disease.

Most of the degenerative illnesses thought to be linked to high blood lipid levels take years (or decades) to develop. Unless an individual is going to stay on a ketogenic consume less calories for extremely long periods of time, it is not thought that there will be appreciable problems with cholesterol build up. From a purely anecdotal stand point, some individuals who have experienced testing show a total lack of cholesterol buildup in their arteries.

Another problem is that weight/fat loss per se is known to decrease cholesterol levels and it is difficult to distinguish the effects of the ketogenic eat less from the effects of the weight/fat loss which happens. A few all around outlined studies allow us to make the following rough generalizations:

1. On the off chance that an individual loses weight/fat on a ketogenic diet, their cholesterol levels will go down.
2. On the off chance that an individual does not lose weight/fat on a ketogenic diet, their cholesterol levels will go up.

Also, there can be a decrease followed by increase in blood lipid levels. This is thought to represent the fact that body fat is a storage facility for cholesterol and the breakdown of body fat during weight misfortune causesa release of cholesterol into the blood stream. Additionally, women may see a greater increase in cholesterol than men while on the ketogenic eat less although the reason for this gender differencein unknown. In practical experience however, there is a great range of responses among individuals on a ketogenic diet.Somes how a drastic decrease in cholesterol while others shown an increase.

Effects on the brain

A well known effect of ketogenic diets is the increased use of ketones by the brain. As well, some of the effects of the ketogenic diet in treating youth epilepsy may be due to this increased extraction of ketones. Due to the changes which occur, a variety of concerns has been voiced in terms of possible side effects. These include change less brain hindrance and short term memory loss.

These concerns are difficult to comprehend in terms of where they originated. What must be comprehended is that ketones are normal physiological substances. As discussed in great detail in the above, ketones provide the brain with fuel when glucose (or food in general) is not available. The brain develops the enzymes to utilize ketones during fetal development and these enzymes are still present as weage, which should serve to illustrate that ketones are normal fuels, and not toxic by products of an unusual metabolism.

Although not a perfect show, epileptic children provide some understanding into conceivable negative long term effects of the ketogenic diet on mind function.Quite simply, there are no negative effects in terms of cognitive function. Except for some initial transient fatigue, similar to what is reported in adults, thereappears to be no decrement in mental functioning while on the diet or after it is ended.

However, this is not absolute proof that the ketogenic diet could not have possible long term effects on the brain, simply that no data currently exists to suggest that it will have any negative impacts. Anecdotally, individuals tend to report one of two sorts of functioning while in ketosis: excellent or terrible. Some individuals feel that they concentrate better and think more lucidly while in ketosis, others feel nothing yet fatigue. Differences in individual physiology may explain the distinction.

With regard to short term memory loss, the only study which remotely addresses this point is a recent study which indicated temporary decrements in a trail making task (which reduires a high degree of mental flexibility) during the first week of a low calorie ketogenic eat less ascompared to a non ketogenic diet. The majority of the effects were seen during the first week of the eat less carbs, and disappeared as the study progressed.

As stated previously, some individuals do note mental fatigue and a lack of concentration amid the first 1 – 3 weeks of a ketogenic diet. In practical terms, this means that individuals who operate heavy machinery, or need maximum mental acuity for some reason (i.e. a presentation or final exam) should not start a ketogenic diet during this time period.

Uric Acid levels

Uric acid is a waste product of protein metabolism that is excreted through the kidneys.Under normal circumstances, uric acid is excreted as quickly as it is produced. This keeps a build up of uric acid in the circulation system which can cause problems, the most common of which is gout. Gout occurs when urate cause deposit in the joints and cause pain.

High levels of uric acid in the blood stream can occur under one of two conditions: when production is increased or when removal through the kidneys is decreased. The ketogenic diet has been shown to affect the rate of uric acid excretion through the kidneys.

Ketones and uric acid contend for the same transport mechanism in the kidneys. Thus when the kidneys remove excess ketone bodies from the blood stream, the removal of uric acid decreases and a build up happens.

Studies of the ketogenic diet and PSMF show a consistent and large (often times doubling or tripling from normal levels) initial increase in uric acid levels in the blood. In general however, levels return towards normal after several weeks of the diet. Small amounts of carbohydrates (5% of add up to dailycalories) can prevent a build up of uric acid. Additionally, in studies of both epileptic kids as well as adults the incidence of gout are very few, and only occur in individuals who are predisposed genetically.

CHAPTER 6: When the Ketogenic Diet Should Not Be Used

While the ketogenic diet is safe for most individuals, there are some people who ought to not follow the diet plan. On the off chance that you havecertain metabolic conditions or health conditions, talk to your doctor before starting a ketogenic diet. Contra indicated health conditions include:

- Gallbladder ailment
- Impaired fat digestion
- History of pancreatitis
- Kidney disease
- Impaired liver function
- Poor nutritional status
- Previous gastric by pass surgery
- Type 1 diabetes
- Impaired insul in production Excessive alcohol use Carnitine deficiency Porphyria

On the other hand, there are other groups of people for whom the ketogenic diet does not posture any serious health risks, however it may not necessarily benefit them, either. For people with metabolic disorders, ketogenic diet spose more risk than benefit and can cause a great deal of harm.On the off chance that you have one of these conditions, or if you drink alcohol excessively, a ketogenic diet is not for you.

Pregnancy
On the off chance that you are pregnant or trying to move toward becoming pregnant, a ketogenic diet may not be right for you. A woman is the most fruitful when her body feels satisfied and well nourished.

Because ketosis is essentially a starvation express, it is a gamble for women trying to become pregnant to try this diet. A high level of ketones in the blood may also pose a risk to a creating fetus. While traditional low carbohydrate diets are okay during pregnancy, you should not limit your carbohydrates to the point of ketosis if you are pregnant. High Intensity Metabolic Conditioning There are some clashing views on whether following a ketogenic diet during periods of intense exerciseis beneficial or not. Some athletes assert that ketosis boosts energy, while others, usually those who do high force exercises such as sprints or Cross Fit workouts, become burned out faster. High intensity exercises require glucose, and although your body can make glucose from protein and fat, it is does not do it at the rate at which you need it to sustain high intensity workouts. Because of this, your body may turn to put away muscle glycogen, which depletes reasonably quickly, and your performance may decrease. When you are burned out and your glycogen stores are depleted, you are more likely to have traded off form and sustain an damage during a workout.

Testing Your Ketone Levels
Once you have entered a state of ketosis, the goal is to stay there. The longer you remain in ketosis, the better your body get sat burning ketones for fuel and the better you will feel.
Testing your ketones will likewise allow you to monitor your ketone levels so that you will know if they are getting too high. You can determine whether you are in ketosis, and monitor your ketone levels, using several different at home test options.

Urine Test,
Most drug stores carry urine strips that measure the sum of ketones in your urine. These urine strips test the pH of your urine and can give you a general thought of the level of ketones, in any case, they have their limitations.

There are three major types of ketones present in the blood when you have reached a state of ketosis: acetoacetate (AcAc) beta hydroxy butyrate (BHB) and CH3)2CO, which is a by product of acetoacetate. Following a few weeks on the ketogenic diet, levels of ketones begin to rise and your body starts to use them as fuel. Once you become keto adapted, which takes another few weeks, the muscles convert AcAc ketones into BHB ketones. So why does this matter? The urine ketone test strips only measure for AcAc ketones, so while they are great for measuring your ketone levels when you are new to a ketogenic diet, they might not give you an accurate picture as your body becomes adapted to using ketones as fuel.

Additionally, as you become keto adapted and your body begins to efficiently use ketones as fuel, you will excrete fewer ketones in your urine. This means that a pee ketone test may demonstrate no ketones at all even though you are really in the optimal state of ketosis. Changes in hydration status also affect the amount of ketones in your urine. A high water intake will lower the concentration of ketones in the urine. Because it is important to stay well hydrated on a ketogenic diet, you may see numbers that do not give you an accurate picture.

Blood Test
Because urine testing is not as accurate over the long term, many people who are serious about staying in ketosis have turned to blood meters to test ketones. To test your blood ketone levels, you will prick your finger with a lancet, which is included in the blood meter kit, and then place a drop of blood on a specialized testing strip. The testing strip goes into the blood meter and gives you a reading on the screen.

Interpreting the Numbers
It is best to measure your blood ketone levels in the morning on a empty stomach since certain things for case, a high fat meal can affect the reading. A blood ketone level of below 0.5 mmol/L

(millimolesper liter) is not considered ketosis. Once you reach a blood ketone level of 0.5 mmol/L to 1.5 mmol/L, you have entered a stateof light nutritional ketosis. Here it is likely that you will experience some weight loss, yet the effects won't be optimal. Optimal ketosisis defined as having a blood ketone level of 1.5 mmol/L to 3.0 mmol/L. This is the state suggested for maximum fat burning. Ketone levels higher than 3.0 mmol/L are not necessary, and this is where ketosis has the potential to become dangerous. There is also anecdotal evidence that having a ketone level higher than the optimal range may really inhibit fat loss.

When to Test
When you test your ketone levels is at least as important as the method you use to test. Because ketone levels fluctuate through out the day and after meals, you have to be strategic about when you test to get an accurate reading. High fat meals, especially those that contain a lot of medium chain triglycerides, will have a direct effect on ketone levels, so avoid testing immediately after meals. Intense aerobic exercise will also increase ketone levels. As a general rule, ketone levels tend to be bring down in the morning than in the evening because of all the fat you eat amid the day. Testing in the morning right when you wake up may give you the most accurate results.
For the most accurate long term results, it is a good idea to test your ketone levels around the same time every day. On the off chance that you have trouble remembering, set an caution on your cell telephone or write yourself a note by your bed side to test your levels right when you wake up.

Staying Safe and Achieving Success
Once you and your health care provider have decided that a ketogenic diet is right for you, there are a number of things you can do to ensure that you not only achieve your goals yet also stay safe on the diet plan.

Eat Enough
A ketogenic diet is not about excessively restricting calories. Although you do need to stay with in a certain caloric range depending on your individual characteristics, you always want to make sure you are eating enough. Restricting carbohydrates and calories too much can leave you feeling tired and moody and can hinder your weight loss progress.
A ketogenic diet is not about starving yourself, it is about providing yourself with all of the calories and nutrients you need while restricting carbohydrate in take. As you lose weight, you may have to adjust the amount of calories you need, so make sure to monitor your progress and re evaluate your diet plan whe never necessary.

Vary Your Food Choices
As with anyother diet plan, varying your food choices as much aspossible will help ensure that you are getting all of the nutrients you require to stay healthy. In the event that you eat the same thing over and over, day after day, you may not be getting a certain vitamin or mineral that you need. A ketogenic diet is more restrictive than other diet plans, however that does not mean you do not have options. Familiarize yourself with your options and vary your plate as much as possible.

Consider Supplements
Many people can get all of the nutrients they need through a balanced ketogenic count calories. However, some individuals may need supplementation with specific supplements. This largely depends on individual characteristics. In the event that you feel that you are doing everything right, however you still do not feel great on a ketogenic diet, contact a functional prescription practitioner or a functional nutritionist. These human services practitioners will be able to do the fitting testing to determine if you have any nutritional inadequacies or identify

any areas where your eat less carbs may be lacking. Based on this information, a functional medicine practitioner will be able to recommend specific supplements foryou.

There are certain supplements that tend to be the most popular for people following a ketogenic diet. Leucine and lysine are two amino acids that help support ketosis and allow you a little more wiggle room with your protein intake. Although vitamin D levels tend to be low in the American population as a whole, those who follow a ketogenic diet may be at a higher risk of becoming deficient. Taking coconut oil as a supplement, 1 to 2 tablespoonsper day, can help you reach your fat goals and help prevent constipation while on the diet.

CHAPTER 7: Troubleshooting Constipation

Constipation is a common concern for those on a ketogenic diet, especially those who are in the beginning times. On the off chance that you are experiencing obstruction on a ketogenic diet, there are some steps you can take to get things moving again.

In addition to taking 1 to 2 tablespoons of coconut oil each day, drink adequate sums of water (half of your body weight in ounces). On the off chance that you are 200 pounds, this implies Bowel movements are extremely important because they permit the body to kill waste and prevent toxins from accumulating in the body. You should be having a bowel development at least once a day, although once after every meal is ideal.

100 ounces of water every day. You additionally need to make sure you are getting enough salt, which helps maintain water balance and replenish sodium levels. Constipation may likewise be a sign that your protein in take is too high and your fat consumption is not high enough.

Achieving success on a ketogenic diet may take some trial and error and a little bit of hone, yet once you get into the routine and reach a state of optimal ketosis, your body will adjust accordingly. In the event that you experience any awkward symptoms or hit any road blocks, contact a functional medicine doctor or a functional nutritionist who can help you troubleshoot and over come any hurdles.

Foods to Eat and Avoid

When following a ketogenic diet, some foods are strictly beyond reach, while others fall into a sort of grayarea. Not with standing of whether foodsare "allowed," you still have to make sure that you are staying inside your macronutrient ratios. Just because a food is technically allowed does not mean you can eat as much of it as you want. Use these suggestions as a rule, yet always make sure that you are staying with in your computed macronutrient ratios.

A Word on Quality
The quality of your sustenance matters, especially when it comes to fat and protein sources.

Ideally, you want to choose meats that are organic, grass fed, and field raised. Eggs should come from your local farmer or from pasture raised hens whenever possible.

Choose grass fed butter and organic creams, cheese, fruits, and vegetables. Eating conventional nourishments won't prevent you from entering a ketogenic state, yet high quality sustenances are better for your body in general. After all, you are what you eat. Do your best to get the most astounding quality food you can find and or afford.

Fats and Oils
Fats and oils provide the basis of your ketogenic diet, so you will want to make sure you are eating plenty of them. The ketogenic diet is not just a fat free for all, though. While following a ketogenic diet, there are certain fats that are better for you than others, although which ones fall into which category may surprise you. On the ketogenic diet, you should eat plenty of saturated fats in the form of meat, poultry, eggs, butter, and coconut, mono unsaturated fats, such as olive oil, nuts, nut butters, and avocado, and natural poly unsaturated fats, such as tuna, salmon, and mackerel. Avoid highly processed polyunsaturated fats, such as canola oil, vegetable oil, and soybean oil. Home made Mayonnaise is likewise an easy way to add a dose of fat to every meal.

Proteins
Many of the fat sources mentioned previously meat, poultry, eggs, butter, nuts, nut butters, and fish are also loaded with

protein and should be your main protein sources when following a ketogenic diet. Bacon and sausage are other sources of protein that also give a significant dose of fat. When eating protein make sure to stay within your recommended grams for the day, since your body turns excess protein into glucose, which can kick you out of ketosis.

Fruits And Vegetables
When following a ketogenic diet, most fruits fall onto the "do not eat" list. Even though the sugars in fruit are natural sugars, they still raise your blood glucose levels significantly and can kick you out of ketosis. There is not a hard rule that fruit is not allowed on a ketogenic diet, yet you do need to limit your intake. When you do eat fruit, choose fruits that are high in fiber and lower in carbohydrates, such as berries, and limit your portions.

Vegetables are extremely essential on a ketogenic diet. They provide the vitamins and minerals that you need to stay healthy and help fill you up without contributing a lot of calories to your day. You do have to be selective about which vegetables you eat, however, since some are loaded with carbohydrates and do not have a place on a ketogenic diet. As a general govern, choose dark green or leafy green vegetables, such as spinach, broccoli, cucumbers, green beans, lettuce, and asparagus. Cauliflower and mushrooms are also good choices for a ketogenic diet. Maintain a strategic distance from starchy vegetables, including white potatoes, sweet potatoes, yams, and corn.

Dairy
Full fat dairy products are a staple on the ketogenic diet. Use butter, heavy cream, sour cream, cream cheese, hard cheese, and cottage cheese to help meet your fat needs. Avoid low fat dairy products and flavored dairy products, such as fruity yogurt.

Flavored yogurt is full of sugar, serving for serving, some versions contain as much sugar and carbohydrates as soda.

Beverages
As with any diet plan, when it comes to refreshments, water is your best bet. Make sure to drink at minimum half of your body weight in ounces. Coffee and tea are also permitted on a ketogenic diet, however they must be unsweetened or sweetened with an approved sweetener, such Stevia or Erythritol. Avoid sodas, flavored waters, sweetened teas, sweetened lemonade, and fruit juices. You can infuse plain water with fresh herbs, such as mint or basil, to give your self a little variety.

Grains And Sugars
Maintain a strategic distance from grains and sugars in all of their forms on the ketogenic diet. Grains include wheat, barley, rice, rye, sorghum, and anything made from these products. That means no breads, no pasta, no saltines, and no rice. Sugar, and anything that contains sugar, is likewise not allowed on a ketogenic diet. This includes white sugar, brown sugar, honey, maplesyrup, corn syrup, and brown rice syrup. There are many names for sugar on ingredient lists, it is extremely beneficial to familiarize yourself with these names so you will know when a product contains sugar in anyform.

Intermittent Fasting on the Ketogenic Diet
Intermittent fasting has recently gained notoriety as a supplement to your diet plan. The basic premise behind irregular fasting is that you can over come a weight loss plateau by completely restricting all food intake for a certain period of time. It is believed that when you deny your body food, your body has to break down stored fat for energy instead. There area few different types of intermittent fasting.

The first is simply skipping meals. Many people who decide to incorporate intermittent fasting into their ketogenic diet plan stop eating after dinner and skip over breakfast to extend the period of time that the body goes without food. Another form of intermittent fasting is giving yourself certain "eating windows. "A eating window is a period of time that you allow yourself to eat, the rest of the time you spend fasting. A typical eating window is between 4 and 7 hours, so you may decide that you will eat all of your meals between 2 p.m. and 7 p.m. and then you do not eat outside of these windows. The last, and most outrageous, form of discontinuous fasting is to completely avoid food for 24 to 48 hours. This is an extreme form of discontinuous fasting and is not recommended. Some people incorporate intermittent fasting every day and others do it once or twice per week.

Although there are narrative reports that intermittent fasting can help ketogenic dieters overcome a weight loss plateau, this has not yet been scientifically proven. On the off chance that you do choose to incorporate intermittent fasting into your ketogenic diet, you may have to play around with it to judge whether or not it works for you. Consult a ?ualified human services professional before incorporating intermittent fasting into your eating routine, especially if you havean existing medical condition.

Starting a Ketogenic Diet

In the event that you are used to following a standard American diet on which most of your calories come from carbohydrates a ketogenic diet is a major change. You have two choices: jump into it cool turkey or slowly wean yourself off carbohydrates, increasing your fat intake until your macronutrient proportions fall inside your goal. When you go into it cold turkey, you are more likely to experience unpleasant carbohydrate withdrawal symptoms, so easing into it gradually is frequently the best bet for success.

Carbohydrate Guides
Carbohydrate guides are a helpful tool to use with the ketogenic diet, especially when you are just starting out. Many books are available that provide a list of nourishments and their carbohydrate count (as well as their calorie, protein, and fat content). Some of these books categorize sustenances into high-carbohydrate, medium carbohydrate, and low carbohydrate lists. There are also several mobile apps that do the same thing.
Whatever method you choose, make sure you have your carbohydrate guide handy when you are food shopping so you can double check what foods are permitted on the eating routine and which foods are not. As you get the hang of the diet, you won't need to check every single food before you purchase it, however it is till handy to have the guides easily accessible for those once in a while foods that you are unsure about.

Prepare Your Kitchen
Once you have made the decision to start a ketogenic consume less calories, you need to prepare your kitchen. This is a two section process: you will need to remove off plan foods and stock your refrigerator and pantry with the essentials. On the off chance that you live alone or with others who are also following a ketogenic diet, removing off plan foods is simple. Go through your wash room and refrigerator and take out all the foods that do not fit into your diet plan. Do not forget to check the labels on your spices and dried herbs. Sometimes these contain sugar or other counterfeit ingredients that do not belong on a ketogenic diet. Donate unopened items to your local food pantry and toss the open ones in the trash.
On the off chance that you are the only one in your house hold starting a ketogenic diet, this removal processis a little more complicated. Instead of giving or throwing out foods that are off plan, divide the pantry up. In the event that possible, put all ketogenic approved foods in a separate cabinet and make it a

point to only go in there and not even look in the off plan cabinet. Dividing up the fridge might beeven more difficult than dividing the store room, yet do the best you can to separate what you can eat from what you can not.

The second part of preparing your kitchen is to stock upon all the essentials. It is imperative that you always have foods on hand that you can eat. On the off chance that you do not, you are more likely to get to the point of being so hungry that you will eat anything. Familiarize yourself with the basics recorded in keep your kitchen supplied with the mat all times.

Ease Into It
When you are excited about starting another diet, it is tempting to jump right in, yet your body will thank you if you ease it into the ketogenic diet slowly. Doing so will lessen these verity of any of the "keto influenza" symptoms you may experience and make the transition a little easier. Give yourself about three to four weeks from the time you commit to following a ketogenic diet to the day you actually start it 100 percent. Although artificially sweetened beverages are allowed on a ketogenic diet because they do not contain any carbohydrates, try to avoid them. Some investigate shows that even though artificial sweeteners do not contain any calories, they can add to weight gain. Plus, part of the goal is to try to get rid of your sweet tooth and drinking sweetened beverages won't help you do that.

Amid the first week, cut out all sugary refreshments. This includes soda, lemonade, sweetened teas, and seasoned waters. In the event that you put sugar in your espresso, scale back utilizeone teaspoon instead of two. After one week of this, expel all desserts and sugary snacks from your eat less, including candy, treats, cakes, muffins, chocolates, and ice cream. Get in the habit of not having dessert after dinner. You want to train your body to stop needing sweets and one way to do this is to cut them out completely, especially while you are transitioning to a ketogenic diet. On your third week, cut out starchy carbohydrates such as pasta, pizza, bread, crackers, rolls, and potatoes. At this point, you may have already started to lose weight.

When you start week 4, you will be ready to formally start your ketogenic eat less. This is when you should start tracking your macronutrients to make sure you are staying with in the adjust ratios. Constraining carbohydrates is important, yet it is not the only goal, make sure you are also eating plenty of fat and moderate amounts of protein.

Approximately 10 percent of individuals will have a seizure at some point in their lifetime. Of those 10 percent, just 30 percent will have a second seizure.

When the seizures occur frequently, and with no known underlying cause, it is called epilepsy.

Stay Hydrated and Replenish Electrolytes

Staying hydrated is always important, however it is especially vital when you are starting a ketogenic diet. It is not only about drinking water, you also need to replenish your electrolytes. When you start a ketogenic diet, you initially lose water, which takes electrolytes such as sodium and potassium with it. Aim to drink the equivalent of at least half your body weight in ounces. This means that, for illustration, if you are 180 pounds, you will want to drink at least 90 ounces of water a day.

You can recharge your electrolytes by drinking a cup of home made bone broth every day, including salt to your foods, and drinking waters that are enhanced with electrolytes.

Just make sure that the enhanced waters are unflavored, as the seasoned water soften contain a lot of sugar and other artificial ingredients.

Planning Meals for Long Term Success

Planning your meals is vital to your long term successon a ketogenic diet. There is a popular quote, most often credited to Benjamin Franklin, that goes something like this: "When you fail to plan, you plan to fail." It is true. The best way to ensure success is to design your weekly meals, prepare meals in advance, and always make sure you have ketogenic approved snacks on hand.

Meal Planning

Take one night a week and write out everything you will eat all week. Plan your suppers and your snacks and afterward gather a grocery list for what you will require in order to execute these dinners and snacks. You may choose to make your meal planning day your shopping day, as well. Get everything you need in one swoop and then do no stray from your plan.

Meal Preparation

Once you know what you are going to eat all week, you may decide that you want to cook each meal individually, or you may decide that spending a few hours preparing your meals makes more sense for you. On the off chance that you choose the last mentioned, pick a day when you do not have any other commitments and spend a few hours in the kitchen preparing your dinners for the entire week. You can make a quiche, a couple of ketogenic friendly goulashes, and a big pot of soup. Partition each supper into to go compartments and store them in the refrigerator so that they are ready to go when you are.

Being Prepared

When you are on a specialized diet such as the ketogenic one, there is really no such thing as convenience foods. You have to be arranged at all times. You might have to take meals and snacks with you every where you go, however it is a small price to pay for the way you will feel. Pack a lunch every day and keep non perishable snacks, like fat bombs, coconut shavings, nuts, and seeds in your auto, in your desk at work, and in your purse or attaché.

Do not Make It Complicated

It is enticing to want to create elaborate meal plans that feature a new gourmet entrée each night, however for most people that is just not realistic. You have to make sure that your new diet plan can fit into your lifestyle, otherwise you won't be ready to stick to it. Keep things basic by eating the same thing for breakfast three times a week and using remains from dinner for the next day's lunch. You can double or triple recipes to prepare meals in mass and then freeze them for another day when you do not have the time to cook.

Starting a new diet is not easy, it takes dedication and preparation. You will have to do some fine tuning and rearranging to figure out what works for you, however once you get the hang of it, it will progress toward becoming second nature.

Keto Fat Bombs

There are hundreds of Ketogenic recipes on the market and on the internet it's for you to choose that suit your taste for your breakfast, lunch and dinner. In the next page of this book we offer our favorite keto fat bombs recipes. It is very convenient that can be eaten in many ways you want that give you extra fuel throughout the day as a meal replacement, quick breakfast and mid-afternoon snacks.

Keto Fat Bombs are typically shape in small balls or bite size of low-carb, high fat treats and fun snacks. Since it's handy it become popular for people that into ketogenic diet. Can be either sweet or savory filled with healthy fats. These are different from energy or protein balls as these fat bombs prioritize fat over protein. Many reports that fat bombs give them extra boost of energy during pre-workout or post- workout that help fight cravings for hours. Make sure you are using ingredients that are low in carb and sugar-free.

Fight Carb and Sugar Cravings
Carb cravings usually occur at the beginning of your keto. Your body need to adopt to it and it's true that struggle is too real. Slowly minimize your carbs carbs until you reach that your body already can adopt to it. Make sure you are drinking lots of fluids as your body are flushing water that make you feel dehydrated.

Sugar Cravings while in keto diet is completely normal it may take a while to adjust. Dealing with sweet cravings by chewing sugar-free gum, coffee or teas (caffeinated is fine) and by drinking water. Sometimes cravings confuse with thrist so make sure you are drinking plenty of water for at least 8 cups a day.

Common Keto Fat Bombs Ingredients
Good Fats

Saturated Fats: Red Meat, Butter, Ghee, Lard, Cream, Eggs, Coconut oil (MCTs), Cocoa butter, Plam oil.
Monounsaturated Fats: Extra virgin olive oil, Avocados, Avocado oil, Nut oil and Bacon fat.
Natural Polyunsaturated Fats: Can be found in Fish, Fish oil, flaxseed and Chia seeds
Natural Trans Fat: can be found in meat of grass-fed animals and dairy products

Avoid the Bad Fats
Processed Polyunsaturated Fats: Vegetable and Seeds oil like Soybean, Canola, Peanut, Sunflower, Sesame and Grapeseed oil.
Processed Trans Fats: Processed foods, margarine, commercially baked goods, and Fast Foods.

Flavouring you can use also sugar-free vanilla extract, cacao powder, 100% dark chocolate, salt, peppermint, lemon, and spices (cayenne, cinnamon, ginger and many more) As nuts and seeds are high in fats and protein you can easily add on to the recipe.
Take note that keto diet must be sugar-free but there are recipes wouldn't possible not to add on sugar. Luckily, there are keto friendly sweeteners that you can substitute. These keto sugars like Erythritol, Natvia, Xylitol, Swerve, Monk fruit (Lakanto sweetener) and Stevia (the most popular sugar substitute) are readily available, just take a look at your favorite grocery baking aisle.

Why Fat Bombs?
The challenges in making full ketogenic meal are lack of time to prepare and the inability to finish the full meal. While Keto fat bombs is an easy solution in ketogenic diet. As they are small portion, quick to make and very easy to consume, it can decrease the time in food preparation. You can make in bulk in

one large batch, store it in an airtight container and put inside the fridge if you are not eating them. It can last up to 2 weeks.
In the next page follow our 50 favorite Keto Fat Bombs Recipes. Enjoy!

Vanilla Cheesecake Fat Bombs (Serves 18)

Ingredients:

9 ounces of Cream Cheese

2 ounces of Erythritol

2 Teaspoons of Vanilla Extract

1 cup of Heavy Cream

Directions:

1. Put your cream cheese, vanilla and erythritol into your kitchen aid and mix on low. Alternatively put into your bowl and mix with your hand mixer on a low speed for 2 minutes, pausing to scrape down the sides of your bowl with a spatula, so as to achieve a smooth consistent texture.

2. Add half of your heavy cream and mix for another 2 minutes. Allow your bowl to sit for 3 to 5 minutes as erythritol in its granulated form requires a little extra time to dissolve.

3. Add the other half of your heavy cream and mix on a medium speed for 3 minutes until your mixture is thick with firm peaks.

4. Gently spoon your mixture into a piping bag and pipe into mini cupcake liners. Set your fat bombs in your refrigerator for at least 1 hour.

5. Serve and Enjoy!

Nutrition Facts:

Calories: 88

Carbs: 1 gram

Red Velvet Fat Bombs (Serves 24)

Ingredients:

3 1/2 ounces of 90% Dark Chocolate (Sugar Free)

3 tablespoons of Natvia

3 1/2 ounces of Butter

4 1/2 ounces of Cream Cheese

1 teaspoon of Vanilla Extract

1/3 cup of Heavy Cream

4 drops of Red Food Coloring

Directions:

1. Melt your chocolate in a heatproof bowl over a small-sized pot of simmering water. Make sure that

your bowl isn't touching the water, as this will cause your chocolate to burn.

2. While your chocolate is melting, mix together your remaining ingredients with a hand mixer on a medium speed for approximately 3 minutes. Ensure the mix is fully combined.

3. With your hand mixer on a low speed, slowly add your chocolate mixture to the other ingredients. Mix on a medium speed for 2 minutes.

4. Add your mixture to a piping bag and pipe the fat bomb mixture onto a lined tray. Set in your refrigerator for approximately 40 minutes.

5. Add your heavy cream to a whipping canister and apply to your fat bombs. (Make sure the cream and canister are cold for a better-whipped cream)

6. Serve and Enjoy!

Nutrition Facts:

Calories: 59

Net Carbs: 1 gram

Vanilla Strawberry Fudge Fat Bombs (Serves 32)

Ingredients:

Vanilla Layer:

8 ounces of Butter

8 ounces of Cream Cheese

2 tablespoons of Erythritol

1 tablespoon of Vanilla Extract

Strawberry Fudge Layer:

8 ounces of Butter

8 ounces of Cream Cheese

1 ounce of Low Carb Strawberry Protein Powder

Directions:

Vanilla Layer:

1. Line your baking tray with parchment paper and set to the side.

2. Place your softened cream cheese, softened butter, vanilla extract, and erythritol in your bowl and mix with your hand mixer on a low speed. Slowly build up to medium-high speed, until all your ingredients are well combined.

3. Pour your vanilla layer into the lined tray and smooth out as evenly as possible. Set in your refrigerator for approximately 30 minutes.

Strawberry Layer:

1. As you did with the vanilla layer, place your softened cream cheese, butter, and strawberry protein powder in your bowl. Mix on a low speed with your hand mixer. Slowly increase your speed to a medium-high until all of your ingredients are well combined.

2. Pour your strawberry layer on top of the vanilla layer, smooth it out and set in your refrigerator for 1 hour.

3. Cut your fudge into bite-sized pieces and keep it cool, as it will soften quickly in warm temperatures.

4. Serve and Enjoy!

Nutrition Facts:

Calories: 150

Carbs: 0.2 grams

Fat: 16 grams

Pina Colada Fat Bombs (Serves 16)

Ingredients:

2 teaspoons of Pineapple Essence

2 tablespoons of Gelatin

3 teaspoons of Erythritol

1/2 cup of Boiling Water

1 teaspoon of Rum Essence

1/2 cup of Coconut Cream

Directions:

1. Dissolve your gelatin and erythritol in your boiling water in a heatproof jug and add your pineapple essence.

2. Allow to cool for 5 minutes.

3. Add your coconut cream and rum extract and continue stirring for 2 minutes.

4. Pour into silicon molds and set for at least 1 hour, depending on the size of your mold.

5. Gently remove from your mold. Store in the refrigerator.

6. Serve and Enjoy!

Nutrition Facts:

Calories: 23

Carbs: 0.4 grams

Fat: 2 grams

Lemon & Poppyseed Fat Bombs (Serves 18)

Ingredients:

8 ounces of Softened Cream Cheese

1 tablespoon of Poppy Seeds

3 tablespoons of Erythritol

4 tablespoons of Sour Cream

2 tablespoons of Lemon Juice

1 Lemon (Zest Only)

Directions:

1. Place all of your ingredients in your bowl and using a hand mixer, mix on a low speed, when your ingredients are combined, mix on medium-high speed for approximately 3 minutes.

2. Gently spoon your mixture into mini cupcake cases or place into a piping bag and pipe into mini cupcakes cases. Refrigerate for at least 1 hour.

3. Serve and Enjoy!

Nutrition Facts:

Calories: 60

Carbs: 1 gram

Fat: 5 grams

Chocolate Kisses Fat Bombs (Serves 24)

Ingredients:

8 ounces of Softened Cream Cheese

1 teaspoon of Vanilla Essence

1/4 cup of Natvia Icing Mix

5 ounces of Sugar-Free Chocolate

7 ounces of Heavy Cream

Directions:

1. Add your chocolate to a small-sized heatproof bowl and place over a small-sized saucepan of simmering water, ensuring that your bowl doesn't touch the water.

2. Melt your chocolate completely and remove from the heat. Set to the side.

3. Place your softened cream cheese in your bowl, using your hand mixer, mix on a medium speed until smooth.

4. Add your Natvia Icing Mix and vanilla essence and mix on a low speed until combined.

5. Add your heavy cream and mix on a medium speed until smooth and beginning to thicken.

6. Pour in your melted chocolate and mix on a medium speed, until all your ingredients are completely combined and the mixture is firm enough to pipe.

7. Add your mixture to a piping bag with a star nozzle. Pipe evenly into mini cupcake papers. Fill 24 cupcake papers, depending on your piping skills, you may get more or less.

8. Cover the kisses and set in your refrigerator for approximately 3 hours, or overnight.

9. They can be stored, covered in your refrigerator for up to 1 week, or frozen for up to 3 months.

10. Serve and Enjoy!

Nutrition Facts:

Calories: 80

Carbs: 4 grams

Fat: 6 grams

Chapter Three: Savory Keto Fat Bomb Recipes

In this section, I will show you 25+ savory ketogenic fat bomb recipes you can cook for yourself. These are keto fat bombs are geared towards people wanting to satisfy their savory side. These recipes are easy to prepare no matter what your level in the kitchen. These delicious treats will help keep you on track with your ketogenic diet.

Pizza Fat Bombs (Serves 6)

Ingredients:

4 ounces of Cream Cheese

8 Pitted Black Olives

14 slices of Pepperoni

2 tablespoons of Chopped Fresh Basil

2 tablespoons of Sun-Dried Tomato Pesto

Salt

Pepper

Directions:

1. Dice your pepperoni and olives into small-sized pieces.

2. Mix together your cream cheese, basil, and tomato pesto.

3. Add your olives and pepperoni into your cream cheese and mix again.

4. Form into balls, then garnish with pepperoni, olive, and basil.

5. Serve and Enjoy!

Nutrition Facts:

Calories: 101

Net Carbs: 1.7 grams

Salmon Fat Bombs (Serves 6)

Ingredients:

1/3 cup of Grass-Fed Butter

1/2 cup of Full-Fat Cream Cheese

1 tablespoon of Fresh Lemon Juice

1/2 package of Smoked Salmon or Smoked Mackerel

1 to 2 tablespoons of Freshly Chopped Dill (Skip if Using Mackerel)

Pinch of Salt

Directions:

1. Place your cream cheese, butter, and smoked salmon into a food processor.

2. Add fresh lemon juice and dill and pulse until smooth. I'm using your mixer with a food processor attachment.

3. Line a tray with parchment paper and create small-sized fat bombs using about 2 1/2 tablespoons of the mixture per piece. Garnish with more dill and place in your refrigerator for 1 to 2 hours or until firm.

4. Alternatively, simply spoon the mixture into an airtight container. Eat immediately or store in your refrigerator for up to a week. When ready to be served,

just spoon out about 2 1/2 tablespoons per serving. Eat on top of crunchy lettuce leaves.

5. Serve and Enjoy!

Nutrition Facts:

Calories: 147

Net Carbs: 0.7 grams

Salmon Breakfast Bombs (Serves 2)

Ingredients:

Breakfast Bombs:

4 ounces of Sliced Smoked Salmon

2 Large Eggs

2 tablespoons of Chopped Fresh Chives

1/2 tablespoon of Salted Butter

Salt

Pepper

Hollandaise Sauce:

2 tablespoons of Salted Butter

1/4 teaspoon of Dijon Mustard

1 Large Egg Yolk (Separated From the White)

1/2 tablespoon of Water

2 teaspoons of Lemon Juice (Freshly Squeezed)

Salt

Directions:

1. Ensure you have all of your ingredients for hollandaise ready and sitting at room temperature.

2. Grab a small-sized pot and fill with water then put on your stove to boil. Once your water is boiling add your 2 whole eggs and let them boil for 10 to 12 minutes. You want your eggs to be hard boiled as we will be adding hollandaise to these.

3. While you are waiting for your eggs to boil, take your salmon slices and finely dice. Make sure they are separated once cut.

4. Preheat a pan over a high-heat and add your 2 teaspoons of butter. Once your butter has heated up, take approximately half of the cut up salmon and add into your pan then crisp into little crunchy pieces. Set to the side.

5. Once your eggs have boiled for approximately 10 to 12 minutes run your eggs and pot under cold water and allow your eggs to cool before peeling.

6. When your eggs have cooled, place them in a dish and use your fork to finely mash the egg.

7. After you have your eggs and salmon prepared you can make a start on your hollandaise. Don't try and do this at the same time as it will need your full attention to avoid clumps and splitting.

8. Take a pot and fill with a cup or two of water and place on your stove to simmer. Melt your 2 tablespoons of butter in the microwave for 30 to 60 seconds. You want your butter to be melted but not

hot. Set to the side. In a large-sized heat-safe bowl whisk your egg yolk, lemon juice, dijon mustard and a pinch of salt together until you see air bubbles. Place your bowl with egg mixture over your pot with the simmering water to create a double boiler. Make sure that your water does not touch the bottom of the bowl.

9. Use a medium heat and continuously whisk your mixture until it starts to thicken.

10. Once the mixture starts thickening, slowly pour in your melted butter while stirring with a whisk. Ensure you keep stirring the entire time to avoid clumps. Once all of your butter is added, place your bowl back onto the pot to thicken further.

11. When your sauce has fully thickened you can remove it and set to the side. If your sauce is too thick add a tiny bit of water to thin, but remember you want a thick consistency.

12. Allow your hollandaise to cool to room temperature. You don't want to cook the salmon when you add the hollandaise, so it is crucial this is cool.

13. Take the raw salmon. hollandaise, half the chives, and mix well with your mashed egg. This should form a firm mixture.

14. Once combined, split your mixture into four pieces and roll into balls.

15. Mix your remaining chives and the crispy salmon together and roll your bombs in this to coat.

16. Serve and Enjoy!

Nutrition Facts:

Calories: 295

Net Carbs: 1 gram

Salmon and Dill Fat Bombs (Serves 12)

Ingredients:

1 cup of Cream Cheese

1/2 package of Smoked Salmon

2/3 cup of Butter

Lemon Juice (To Taste)

Salt (To Taste)

Dill (To Taste)

Directions:

1. Add all of your ingredients into a food processor and blend.

2. Create small-sized balls with your mixture and pop in your refrigerator.

3. Serve and Enjoy!

Nutrition Facts:

Calories: 174

Bacon Guacamole Deviled Eggs (Serves 6)

Ingredients:

4 strips of Thick Cut Bacon (Cooked Crisp & Crumbled)

6 Large Eggs

1 Large Avocado

1 tablespoon of Minced Garlic

2 tablespoons of Salsa

1 tablespoon of Dried Onion Flakes

1 tablespoon of Lime Juice

1/2 teaspoon of Garlic Salt

Pinch Cayenne Pepper

Directions:

1. Hard boil your eggs. Place your eggs in a large-sized saucepan with cold water. Add enough water that your eggs are fully submerged. Over a high heat bring your water to a rolling boil. Once your water is boiling, remove the pan from the heat, cover and allow it to sit for 12 minutes.

2. In your large-size mixing bowl, fork mash the avocado. Peel your eggs and slice in half lengthwise. Scrape the yolks out into your mixing bowl. To your bowl, add your bacon, salsa, garlic, lime juice, onion

flakes, garlic salt, and cayenne pepper. Mix until all your ingredients are well incorporated.

3. Put your mixture into a plastic bag. Squeeze your mixture to one corner of the bag and snip off the corner of the bag. Use this to pipe the mixture into your eggs.

4. Serve and Enjoy!

Nutrition Facts:

Calories: 140

Net Carbs: 2.8 grams

Bacon Wrapped Mozzarella Sticks (Serves 2)

Ingredients:

1 Frigo Cheese Heads Mozzarella Cheese Stick (Cut In Half)

2 slices of Bacon

Coconut Oil (For Frying)

Low-Sugar Pizza Sauce (Optional)

Toothpicks

Directions:

1. Preheat your coconut oil in your deep fryer to 350 degrees.

2. Wrap your cut in half cheese sticks with your bacon, overlapping as you go just a bit so the bacon stays on. At the end of the wrapping, secure with your toothpick.

3. Drop your bacon wrapped cheese in your hot oil and cook until your bacon is brown and crispy, should take approximately 2 to 3 minutes.

4. Remove to a paper towel to cool for a few minutes. Remove the toothpick and serve with your favorite low-sugar dipping sauce.

5. Enjoy!

Nutrition Facts:

Calories: 103

Net Carbs: 1 gram

Bacon & Guacamole Fat Bombs (Serves 6)

Ingredients:

1/2 Large Avocado

4 Large Slices of Bacon

1/4 cup of Butter or Ghee (Softened at Room Temperature)

2 cloves of Crushed Garlic

1/2 Small Diced White Onion

1 Small Finely Chopped Chili Pepper

1 tablespoon of Fresh Lime Juice

1 to 2 tablespoons of Freshly Chopped Cilantro

1/4 teaspoon of Salt

Freshly Ground Black Pepper

Directions:

1. Preheat your oven to 375 degrees. Line your baking tray with parchment paper. Lay your bacon strips out flat on your parchment paper, leaving space so they don't overlap. Place your tray in the oven and cook for approximately 10 to 15 minutes until golden brown. The time depends on the thickness of your bacon slices. When done, remove from your oven and set to the side to cool down.

2. Halve, deseed and peel your avocado. Place your avocado, crushed garlic, butter, chili pepper, lime juice, and cilantro into your bowl and season with salt and pepper.

3. Mash using a potato masher or a fork until well combined. Add your diced onion and mix well.

4. Pour in your bacon grease from the tray where you baked the bacon and mix well. Cover with your foil and place in the refrigerator for 20 to 30 minutes.

5. Crumble your bacon into small-sized pieces and prepare for "breading." Remove your guacamole mixture from the refrigerator and start creating 6 balls. You can use a spoon or an ice-cream scooper. Roll each ball in your bacon crumbles and place on a tray that will fit in the refrigerator.

6. Serve and Enjoy!

Nutrition Facts:

Calories: 156

Net Carbs: 1.4 grams

Bacon, Pistachio, and Braunshweiger Truffles (Serves 12)

Ingredients:

8 ounces Braunshweiger Liverwurst (Room Temperature)

8 slices of Bacon (Cooked Crisp & Chopped Finely)

1/4 cup of Chopped Pistachio Kernels

1 teaspoon of Dijon Mustard

6 ounces of Softened Cream Cheese

Directions:

1. Combine your Braunshweiger and pistachios in a small-sized food processor and pulse until combined.

2. In a separate small-sized bowl, whip your softened cream cheese and mustard together until smooth.

3. Roll your Braunshweiger into 12 small balls.

4. Then take each ball and form about a 1/4 inch thick layer of cream cheese with your fingers.

5. Once you have done all of them, chill for approximately 30 minutes.

6. Roll each ball in the finely chopped bacon and place on a serving dish.

7. Serve and Enjoy!

Nutrition Facts:

Calories: 145

Net Carbs: 1.5 grams

Egg & Bacon Fat Bombs (Serves 6)

Ingredients:

2 Large Eggs

4 Large Slices of Bacon

2 tablespoons of Mayonnaise

1/4 cup of Softened Butter or Ghee

1/4 teaspoon of Salt

Freshly Ground Black Pepper

Directions:

1. Preheat your oven to 375 degrees. Line your baking tray with parchment paper. Lay your bacon strips out flat on the parchment paper, leaving space so they don't overlap. Place your tray in the oven and cook for approximately 10 to 15 minutes until golden brown. The time depends on the thickness of the bacon slices. When done, remove from your oven and set to the side to cool down.

2. Boil your eggs. Fill a small-sized saucepan with water up to three quarters. Add a good pinch of salt. This will prevent your eggs from cracking. Bring to a boil. Using a spoon or hand, dip each egg in and out of your boiling water - be careful not to get burnt. This will prevent your egg from cracking as the temperature change won't be so dramatic. To get your eggs hard-boiled,

you need approximately 10 minutes. This timing works for large eggs. When done, remove from your heat and place in a bowl filled with cold water. When chilled, peel off the shells.

3. Cut the butter into small-sized pieces and add your peeled and quartered eggs. Mash with a fork.

4. Add your mayonnaise, season with pepper and salt and mix together well. Pour in your bacon grease and combine well. Place in your refrigerator for approximately 20 to 30 minutes or until it's solid and easy to form fat bombs.

5. Crumble your bacon into small-sized pieces and prepare for "breading." Remove your egg mixture from the fridge and start creating 6 balls. You can use a spoon or an ice-cream scooper. Roll each ball in the bacon crumbles and place on a tray that will fit in the refrigerator.

6. Serve and Enjoy!

Nutrition Facts:

Calories: 185

Net Carbs: 0.2 grams

Buffalo Chicken Deviled Eggs (Serves 6)

Ingredients:

6 ounces of Chicken (Cooked & Chopped)

6 Large Eggs (Hard Boiled)

1/4 Small Onion

1/4 cup of Franks Buffalo Wing Sauce

1/4 cup of Blue Cheese Crumbles

2 tablespoons of Blue Cheese Dressing

Chopped Small Rib Celery

Directions:

1. While your eggs are boiling, chop up your chicken and the celery.

2. Peel your eggs and slice in half lengthwise. Scrape your yolks out into a large-sized mixing bowl. To your bowl add the rest of the ingredients except for your onion. Grate the onion over your bowl. The juice from your onion will add a lot of flavor to your mixture.

3. Mix all your ingredients together. Put your mixture into a Ziploc bag. Squeeze the mixture to one corner of the bag and snip off the corner of your bag. Use this to pipe the mixture into your eggs.

4. Serve and Enjoy!

Nutrition Facts:

Calories: 111

Net Carbs: 1.3 grams

Bacon-Wrapped Mini Meatloaves (Serves 4)

Ingredients:

1 pound of Ground Beef

1/4 cup of Coconut Milk

1/2 pound of Bacon (Cut In Small Chunks)

8 strips of Bacon

1/3 cup of Minced Fresh Chives

2 Minced Garlic Cloves

Chopped Fresh Parsley

Freshly Ground Black Pepper

Directions:

1. Preheat your oven to 400 F.

2. In a large-sized bowl, combine your ground beef, bacon chunks, garlic, chives, and your coconut milk. Mix well until all of your ingredients hold together.

3. Season your mixture with freshly ground black pepper. No need to add salt to your mixture since the bacon is already salty enough.

4. Take a medium size muffin tin and place a slice of bacon around the sides of each hole.

5. Fill these same eight holes with your beef mixture.

6. Place in your oven and cook for approximately 30 minutes.

7. Once ready and cool enough to handle, remove your mini meatloaves from the muffin tin and add fresh parsley sprinkled on top.

8. Serve and Enjoy!

Nutrition Facts:

Carbs: 2 grams

Fat: 51 grams

Jalapeno Popper Deviled Eggs w/ Bacon

Ingredients:

6 Large Eggs

6 slices of Bacon (Cooked Crisp & Crumbled)

16 Sliced Pickled Jalapenos (Divided)

2 ounces of Softened Cream Cheese

4 to 6 tablespoons of Mayonnaise

1/4 teaspoon of Smoked Paprika

Directions:

1. Hard boil your eggs. Place your eggs in a large-sized saucepan with cold water. Add enough water that your eggs are fully submerged. Over a high heat bring your water to a rolling boil. Once your water has come to a boil, remove the pan from the heat, cover and allow it to sit for approximately 12 minutes.

2. Chop 4 of the jalapeno slices and set to the side.

3. Peel your eggs and slice in half lengthwise. Remove the yolks and fork mash them in your medium mixing bowl. To your bowl, add bacon, cream cheese, mayonnaise, and chopped jalapenos. Mix until all of your ingredients are well incorporated.

4. Spoon your mixture into a plastic bag or pastry bag. Squeeze the mixture to one corner of your bag and snip off the corner. Use this to pipe the filling into your egg halves.

5. Top each egg with a jalapeno slice. Sprinkle your paprika over top of the eggs.

6. Serve and Enjoy!

Cheesy Jalapeno Fat Bombs (Serves 6)

Ingredients:

3 1/2 ounces of Full-Fat Cream Cheese (Room Temperature)

4 slices of No-Sugar Bacon

1/4 cup of Unsalted Butter or Ghee (Room Temperature)

2 Jalapeño Peppers (Halved, Seeded, & Finely Chopped

1/4 cup of Grated Gruyère Cheese or Cheddar Cheese

Directions:

1. In your bowl, mash together your cream cheese and butter, or process in a food processor until smooth.

2. Preheat your oven to 325 degrees.

3. Line your rimmed baking sheet with parchment paper. Be sure to use a rimmed sheet to contain the bacon fat.

4. Lay your bacon slices flat on the parchment, leaving enough space between so they don't overlap.

5. Place your sheet in the preheated oven and cook for approximately 25 to 30 minutes, or until crispy. The exact amount of cooking time depends on the thickness of bacon slices.

6. Remove from your oven and set to the side to cool. When cool enough to handle, crumble your bacon into a bowl and set to the side.

7. To your cream cheese and butter mixture, add the Gruyère or Cheddar cheese, jalapeños, and bacon grease. Mix well to combine. Refrigerate for approximately 30 minutes to 1 hour, or until set.

8. Divide your mixture into 6 fat bombs and place them on a parchment-lined plate. If serving immediately, roll them in your crumbled bacon until well coated. If serving later, refrigerate without the bacon coating in an airtight container for up to 1 week. Roll the fat bombs in freshly cooked or reheated bacon crumbs just before serving.

9. Serve and Enjoy!

Nutrition Facts:

Calories: 208

Net Carbs: 0.7 grams

Savory Mediterranean Fat Bombs (Serves 5)

Ingredients:

1/4 cup of Softened Butter or Ghee

1/2 cup of Cream Cheese (Full-Fat)

2 to 3 tablespoons of Freshly Chopped Herbs (Basil, Thyme, & Oregano)

4 pieces of Drained Sun-Dried Tomatoes

4 Pitted Olives

5 tablespoons of Grated Parmesan Cheese

2 cloves of Crushed Garlic

1/4 teaspoon of Salt

Freshly Ground Black Pepper

Directions:

1. Cut your butter into small-sized pieces and place in your bowl with the cream cheese. Leave it on a kitchen counter for approximately 20 to 30 minutes to soften. Mash with your fork and mix until well combined. Add your chopped sun-dried tomatoes and chopped olives.

2. Add your freshly chopped herbs, crushed garlic, and season with salt and pepper. Mix well and place in your refrigerator for approximately 20 to 30 minutes to solidify.

3. Remove your cheese mixture from the refrigerator and start creating 5 balls. You can use a spoon or an ice-cream scooper. Roll each ball in the grated Parmesan cheese and place on your plate. Eat immediately or store in your refrigerator in an airtight container for up to a week.

4. Serve and Enjoy!

Nutrition Facts:

Calories: 165

Net Carbs: 1.7 grams

Keto Butter Burgers Fat Bombs (Serves 12)

Ingredients:

1 pound of Ground Beef (85% Lean)

2 ounces of Cheese

3 tablespoons of Butter

Pepper

Salt

Garlic Powder (Optional)

Onion Powder (Optional)

Directions:

1. Preheat your oven to 375 degrees.

2. In a medium-sized bowl, combine your ground beef with your desired amount of salt and pepper. Optionally, add your onion powder and/or garlic powder.

3. Press a small amount of beef (about 1 tablespoon) into the bottom of your non-stick, 12-slot muffin pan so the bottom is fully covered.

4. Add a pat of butter to the top of each piece of beef.

5. Add beef to the top. Press to flatten.

6. Add a small piece of cheese to your beef.

7. Add a final layer of beef. Press to flatten.

8. Place your muffin pan in the oven and bake for approximately 10 minutes.

9. When the baking is complete, turn off your oven and crack the oven door for a few minutes to release the heat (if using a silicone muffin pan, wait approximately 10 minutes).

10. Using a fork, remove each butter burger from your pan and place on your plate.

11. There will be a beef fat/butter combo remaining in your muffin pan. Save this and use it to drizzle on your butter burgers.

12. Serve and Enjoy!

Nutrition Facts:

Calories: 125

Fat: 10 grams

Savory Sesame Fat Bombs (Serves 4)

Ingredients:

4 ounces of Butter (Room Temperature)

1 teaspoon of Sea Salt

2 tablespoons of Sesame Oil

2 teaspoons of Toasted Sesame Seeds

1/4 teaspoon of Chili Flakes

Directions:

1. Start by adding sesame seeds to a dry, hot pan and roast them for a couple of minutes while stirring the entire time; be careful not to burn them. Once they are golden brown and start popping, they are done. Transfer immediately to a plate or shallow bowl and set to the side.

2. Mix your butter, sesame oil, chili flakes, and salt in your small-sized bowl. Place in the refrigerator for approximately 15 minutes or more.

3. Shape your butter mixture into balls the size of walnuts, approximately half an ounce. Roll each ball in the toasted sesame seeds. Store in your refrigerator or freezer.

4. Serve and Enjoy!

Sausage Balls Fat Bombs (Serves 23)

Ingredients:

1 pound of Breakfast Sausage

1 cup of Almond Flour

1 Large Egg

1/4 cup of Grated Parmesan

8 ounces of Cheddar Cheese

2 teaspoons of Baking Powder

1 tablespoon of Butter (or Coconut Oil)

1/4 teaspoon of Salt

Directions:

1. Preheat oven to 350 degrees.

2. Add your eggs and spices to your bowl and beat until well combined.

3. Add all other ingredients to your egg mixture.

4. Using your cookie scoop and your hands roll sausage mixture into 20 to 25 sausage balls.

5. Place sausage balls on a cookie sheet.

6. Bake for approximately 16 to 20 minutes.

7. Store in a sandwich bag or covered bowl in your refrigerator.

8. Serve and Enjoy!

Nutrition Facts:

Calories: 124

Carbs: 1 gram

Bacon Burger Bombs (Serves 12)

Ingredients:

12 slices of Bacon

12 Rounds Raw Sausage Patties (1-Ounce Each)

12 Cubes Smoked Cheddar Cheese (1-Inch)

Cumin (To Taste)

Onion Powder (To Taste)

Pepper (To Taste)

Salt (To Taste)

Directions:

1. Preheat your oven to 350 degrees. Lay out your sausage rounds on a cookie sheet lined with your parchment paper.

2. Dust your sausage with cumin, onion powder, pepper, and salt.

3. Place a piece of cheese in the middle of your sausage rounds.

4. Form a ball around your cheese with the sausage. Roll it in your hands to make a good circle shape.

5. Wrap your bacon around your sausage balls.

6. Bake at 350 degrees for an hour.

7. Serve and Enjoy!

Nutrition Facts:

Calories: 250

Net Carbs: 1.4 grams

Sausage Ball Puffs (Serves 36)

Ingredients:

1 pound of Breakfast Sausage (Drained & Browned)

4 Eggs

4 1/2 tablespoons of Melted Butter & Cooled)

2 tablespoons of Full Fat Sour Cream

1/3 cup of Coconut Flour

2 cups of Sharp Shredded Cheddar Cheese

1/4 teaspoon of Baking Powder

1/4 teaspoon of Salt

Directions:

1. Preheat your oven to 375 degrees and grease your cookie sheet.

2. Combine your melted butter (I cool mine by popping the bowl in the refrigerator for 5 minutes), eggs, salt, and sour cream then whisk together.

3. Add your coconut flour and baking powder to your mixture and stir until combined.

4. Add your drained browned sausage.

5. Stir in your cheese.

6. Drop batter by tightly packed spoonfuls on your greased cookie sheet.

7. Bake for approximately 15 to 18 minutes or until tops are slightly brown.

8. Serve and Enjoy!

Nutrition Facts:

Calories: 89

Carbs: 0.6 grams

Fat: 7 grams

Cheesy Bacon Fat Bombs (Serves 20)

Ingredients:

8 ounces of Mozzarella Cheese

10 slices of Bacon

4 tablespoons of Melted Butter

4 tablespoons of Almond Flour

1 Large Egg

3 tablespoons of Psyllium Husk Powder

1/4 teaspoon of Black Pepper

1/4 teaspoon of Salt

1/8 teaspoon of Onion Powder

1/8 teaspoon of Garlic Powder

1 cup of Oil (For Frying)

Directions:

1. Microwave half of your cheese for 45 to 60 seconds or until it is melted.

2. Microwave butter for 15 to 20 seconds until fully melted, then pour butter into your cheese and egg.

3. Mix together and add psyllium husk, almond flour, and spices. Mix together again and pour dough out onto a silpat.

4. Pretty dough and roll out into a rectangle. Fill your rectangle with the rest of your cheese and fold in half (horizontally), then in half again (vertically).

5. Crimp edges and re-form into a rectangle. Cut out 20 squares from this.

6. Wrap each piece of your dough in half of a piece of bacon tightly, using toothpicks to secure the bacon.

7. Heat oven to 375 degrees, then fry each cheesy bacon bomb for 1 to 3 minutes each.

8. Remove from your oil and allow it to cool on your paper towels.

9. Serve and Enjoy!

Nutrition Facts:

Calories: 93

Net Carbs: 0.65 grams

Sausage & Cream Cheese Fat Bombs (Serves 8)

Ingredients:

1 pound of Uncooked Hot Sausage

1 cup of Shredded Cheddar Cheese

2 cups of Bisquick Baking Mix

8-ounce block of Cream Cheese

Directions:

1. Preheat your oven to 350 degrees.

2. Line your baking sheets with parchment paper.

3. In the bowl of a stand mixer, mix together your sausage and cream cheese.

4. Add in your baking mix and stir until combined.

5. Add in your cheese.

6. Stir until well combined.

7. Scoop up meat mixture and form into 1-inch balls and place on your baking sheet.

8. Once you have them all on the baking sheet, just go back and roll them around in your hands to make them a bit more smooth on the outside. Pop your baking sheet in the refrigerator for approximately 10 minutes.

9. Once they are chilled, bake for approximately 25 minutes.

10. Serve and Enjoy!

Nutrition Facts:

Calories: 357

Carbs: 19 grams

Breakfast Bacon Fat Bombs (Serves 6)

Ingredients:

1 Large Hardboiled Egg

6 Cooked Bacon Slices

1/4 Avocado

6 Cooked Bacon Slices

4 tablespoons of Unsalted or Clarified Butter

1 tablespoon of Mayonnaise

2 tablespoons of Bacon Grease

1 Serrano Pepper (Seeded & Diced)

1 tablespoon of Chopped Cilantro

1/4 Juice of Lime

Kosher Salt (To Taste)

Cracked Pepper (To Taste)

Directions:

1. In your large-sized bowl, combine your hardboiled egg, butter, avocado, serrano pepper, mayonnaise, and cilantro. Mash into a smooth paste with your fork or potato masher. Season with salt and pepper, then add your lime juice and stir.

2. Prepare your bacon in your favorite fashion until crispy, reserving 2 tablespoons of bacon grease. Add your bacon grease to the fat bomb mixture and stir gently. Cover and place in your refrigerator for 30 minutes, or until the mixture has cooled and can form solid balls. Crumble your bacon into small bits in a small-sized bowl.

3. Using your spoon, scoop out 6 even-sized amounts of your fat bomb mixture and form into balls. Add the balls to your bacon bits and roll around until completely covered.

4. Serve and Enjoy!

Baked Brie & Pecan Prosciutto Fat Bombs (Serves 1)

Ingredients:

1/2 ounce of Prosciutto

1/8 teaspoon of Black Pepper

6 Pecan Halves

1-ounce Full-Fat Brie Cheese

Directions:

1. Preheat oven to 350 degrees. Use your muffin tin, whose muffin holes are about 2.5 inch wide and 1.5 inch deep.

2. Take the prosciutto and fold it in half so it becomes almost square.

3. Place it in a hole of the muffin tin to line it completely.

4. Chop your Brie in little cubes, leaving the white skin on. Place your Brie in the prosciutto-lined cup.

5. Stick your pecan halves in amongst the Brie.

6. Bake for approximately 12 minutes, until your Brie is melted and prosciutto is cooked.

7. Allow it to cool for approximately 10 minutes before removing from the muffin pan.

8. Serve and Enjoy!

Nutrition Facts:

Calories: 183

Net Carbs: 0.4 grams

Pepperoni Pizza Fat Bombs (Serves 6)

Ingredients:

3 1/2 ounces of Cream Cheese (Room Temperature)

1 clove of Minced Garlic

12 Pepperoni Slices

1/2 Finely Chopped Small Red Pepper

1/3 cup of Grated Parmesan Cheese

1/4 cup of Unsalted Butter (Room Temperature)

1/4 cup of Grated Mozzarella Cheese

2 tablespoons of Chopped Fresh Herbs (Basil, Oregano, or Thyme)

1/8 teaspoon of Chili Powder

Pinch of Salt

Directions:

1. In your bowl, mash together your cream cheese and the butter with a fork, or process in a food processor until smooth.

2. In a large-sized skillet, set over a medium heat, cook your pepperoni slices on both sides until crispy. Transfer to your plate to cool.

3. Add the garlic and red pepper to the pepperoni juices in the skillet and cook for a few minutes over a medium heat until fragrant. Remove from the heat and cool slightly. Add to your cream cheese and butter mixture and mix well with an electric beater or a hand whisk.

4. Add your grated mozzarella cheese, salt, herbs, and chili powder. Mix well again. Refrigerate for 20 to 30 minutes, or until set.

5. Using a large spoon or an ice cream scoop, divide the mixture into 6 balls. Roll each ball in your Parmesan cheese and place on top of 2 slices of crisped pepperoni. Refrigerate in an airtight container for up to 5 days.

6. Serve and Enjoy!

Bacon Wrapped Chicken Bombs (Serves 6)

Ingredients:

2 pounds of Boneless, Skinless Chicken Breasts

4 ounces of Softened Cream Cheese

10 ounces of Frozen Spinach

12 slices of Bacon

1/2 cup of Full-Fat Ricotta

Pepper

Salt

Directions:

1. Thaw your spinach out and wring as much water out of it as possible. Preheat your oven to 375 degrees.

2. Mix your spinach with the cream cheese and full fat ricotta. Season with your salt and pepper.

3. Cut your chicken breasts in half. You want them to still be thick enough to cut pouches into.

4. Carefully cut pockets into one of the ends of each piece of chicken. If you accidentally cut through all the way a little filling might squeeze out, but it's not a big deal. Stuff the pockets with your cheese filling.

5. Tightly wrap two slices of your bacon around each piece of chicken. Try and seal up the open end and any holes where filling might seep out. However, don't wrap it so tight that the chicken folds in on itself or you might have difficulty cooking it through.

6. Pan sear the bacon wrapped chicken in a hot skillet. You don't have to brown all the sides equally, because they will be finished off in the oven.

7. Set your pieces of chicken into an oven safe dish while you finish the others.

8. Bake for approximately 35 to 45 minutes until the bacon is well crisped and the chicken is cooked all the way through. The chicken is done when it reaches 165 degrees.

9. Serve and Enjoy!

Nutrition Facts:

Calories: 385

Net Carbs: 2.3 grams

Conclusion

You tried all kinds of diet and yet still difficult for you to achieved your ideal weight goals. Good thing about this Keto diet not only improve your cholesterol, blood pressure and blood sugar. Studies shows that low-carb diet not only causes more weight loss but also leads to major improvements that reduce appetite and calorie intake.

Keto diet can lose weight faster that those low-fat diets, it is effective in losing harmful abdominal fat or belly fat which is toxic. It is not like the subcutaneous fat on the rest of your body. This is very different fat. It contains inflammatory proteins that cause your arteries to clog up. You're at great risk of having a heart attack or a stroke. You have to get rid of it fast or your chances of reaching old age will be severely diminished.

If you had not thought of losing your belly fat before, now there are some compelling reasons why it is very important that you think of doing so now. It is not just about your looks, or about what the scales tell you every morning, it is about something a bit more serious than that.

That's why we are going Keto as our body become efficient at burning fat for fuel. We are losing stubborn belly fats thru ketosis by limiting the maximum consumption of carbohydrates. The body more readily burns the fat it has stored and resulting in more weight loss.

Ketogenic plan and some exercise studies shows that it has been successful in guiding people not only with slimmer waistline but a better health.

You should take action now. Do whatever you do, rush into a diet without giving it some thought, but you need to plan to change your eating and lifestyle habits so that your belly goes away, and it does not come back.

Part 2

Introduction

The ketogenic diet is an excellent thing. It helps you to drop weight without having to workout.

When you're on a keto diet, one of the most important things you have to do is keep up with your macros. If you cannot get full meals in at least three times a day, then you need to figure out other ways to fill your macro requirements. This is where a lot of *fat bombs and snacks stand in good stead.*

Fat bombs are also very helpful because fats are one of the hardest elements to fill when looking at your macros.

If you happen to be fighting with hitting your macros, making fat bombs can significantly help you with your needs.

You have to eat more fat than anything. Fat bombs give you a big boost of fat that you are going to need.

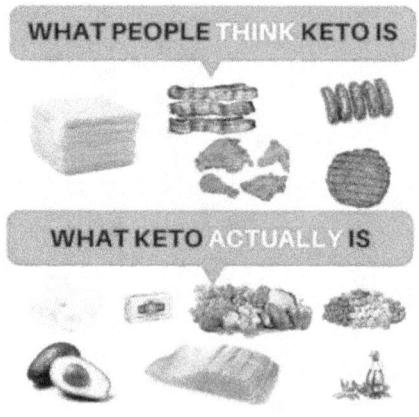

It's curious that many of us spent years escaping fat at all costs when, these days, we're understanding more all the time about the advantages of a low-carb diet, high-fat - keto diet. In this diet, 70 - 80 % your daily calories come from fat, 15 - 20 % is protein and just the remainder, about 5 %, comes from carbohydrates. For many of us, it's a massive shift in how we were brought up eating.

When you are on a high-fat diet, then keto fat bombs are about to be your new favorite snack. So what are fat bombs? They're like energy balls. But instead of relying on the carbs that make up the mass of energy treats, like grains or rice, fat bombs are packed with fat. They're usually made up of about 80 % fat, making them handy for a quick breakfast, pre- or post-workout snack or a little afternoon treat.

But what if you're not on the keto diet? You can still enjoy keto fat bombs! Healthy fats should even make up between 20 - 30 % of your food and a fat bomb is an excellent way to get those calories in. Bonus: Because fats break down more slowly in the digestive tract, they can keep you feeling full for longer!

Keto fat bombs are pretty straightforward. You'll want a mix of healthy fats, like nut butter, avocado, coconut oil, cheese or butter, a low-carb flavor of some sort (think cacao powder or spices) and perhaps a low-carb ingredient that adds texture, like nuts or seeds. Whether you're keto or not, you'll love these bombs!

Keto in a Nutshell

Ketogenic, or keto, is a style of eating that uses weight-based ratios to determine what is eaten in a given meal. Rates are calculated as total weight of fat vs. total weight of carbohydrates plus protein.

It is a low-carb diet, which turns the body into a fat-burning machine. It has many proven advantages for weight loss, health and performance, as millions of people, have experienced already.

What "keto" means?

The "keto" in a ketogenic diet comes from the fact that it makes the body produce small fuel molecules called "ketones".

This is an alternative fuel for the body, used when glucose (blood sugar) is in short supply.

Ketones are produced if you eat minimal carbs (that are instantly broken down into blood sugar) and balanced quantity of protein (excess protein can also be transformed into blood sugar).

Ketones are produced from fat in the liver. Then they are used as fuel everywhere in the body, especially in the brain. The brain is a hungry organ that spends lots of energy each day, and it can't run on fat directly. But it can run on glucose… or ketones.

On a keto diet, your whole body switches its fuel supply to run almost only on fat. Insulin levels become very low, and fat burning increases greatly. It becomes easy to access your fat stocks to burn them off. This is great if you're trying to lose weight, but there are also other less obvious benefits, such as less hunger and a steady supply of energy, keeping you alert and focused.

Benefits of the ketogenic diet:

- Weight loss (fat loss)
- Better sleep
- Elimination of cravings
- All meat and fish, preferably grass-fed, non-medicated meat and wild fish
- Stable moods
- Reduction of risk of many inflammatory and degenerative diseases, (much research has already been done on the benefits of this diet for diabetes, cancer, cardiovascular disease, epilepsy, Alzheimer's and Parkinson's diseases)

Keto foods
- Non-starchy vegetables that grow above ground (especially green leafy vegetables)
- Fats and oils from natural sources like animal fats, grass-fed butter, avocados, coconut oil, coconut milk, olive oil, cacao butter, avocado oil
- Small quantities of low sugar fruits – berries, lemons, limes, avocados
- Nuts and seeds

A Complete Keto Diet Food Guide to Follow

Protein

Liberally:

- Dark meat chicken
- Grass-fed beef

- Fish, especially fatty fish, like salmon

Occasionally:

- Low-fat proteins, like shrimp and skinless chicken breast.
- Bacon

Never:

- Fish or chicken nuggets
- Meat that has been marinated in sugary sauces
- Cold cuts with added sugar

Oil and Fat

Liberally:

- Olive oil
- Coconut oil
- Avocado oil
- Heavy cream
- Butter

Occasionally:

- Corn oil
- Sunflower oil
- Safflower oil

Never:

- Artificial trans fats
- Margarine

Fruits and Veggies

Liberally:

- Leafy greens, like spinach and arugula
- Avocado

- Asparagus
- Celery

Occasionally:

- Spaghetti squash
- Eggplant
- Leeks

Never:

- Raisins
- Potatoes
- Corn

Nuts and Seeds

Liberally:

- Flax and chia seeds
- Almonds
- Walnuts

Occasionally:

- Unsweetened nut butter (almond or peanut butter)
- Pistachios
- Cashews

Never:

- Chocolate-covered nuts
- Sweetened nut or seed butter
- Trail mixes with dried fruit

Dairy Products

Liberally:

- Blue cheese
- Feta cheese

- Cheddar cheese

Occasionally:

- Full-fat plain Greek yogurt
- Full-fat ricotta cheese
- Full-fat cottage cheese

Never:

Milk

- Ice cream
- Sweetened nonfat yogurt

Sweeteners

Liberally: Practice moderation with sweeteners.

Occasionally:

- Erythritol
- Xylitol
- Stevia

Never:

- Honey
- White and brown sugars
- Agave
- Maple syrup

Condiments and Sauces

Liberally:

- Lemon butter sauce
- Mayonnaise (ensure there's no sugar added)
- Guacamole

Occasionally:

- Balsamic vinegar
- Tomato sauce (look for those with no added sugar)
- Raw garlic

Never:

- Barbecue sauce
- Honey mustard
- Ketchup

Drinks

Liberally:

- Water
- Almond milk
- Plain tea
- Bone Broth

Occasionally:

- Zero-calorie drinks
- Black coffee (watch caffeine consumption)
- Unsweetened carbonated water (limit only if bubbles make you bloated)

Never:

- Lemonade
- Soda
- Fruit juice

Herbs and Spices

Liberally: All herbs and spices fit in a keto diet

- Salt
- Pepper
- Cayenne, thyme, oregano, and paprika

Occasionally:

- Onion powder
- Garlic powder
- Ground ginger

Never:

Herbs and spices are generally okay to use in small amounts to add flavor to foods.

Basic principles

1. Ideally, macronutrient ratios should be 60-75% of calories from fat (or more depending on your target), 15-30% calories from protein and 5-10% calories from carbohydrates (net carbs).

2. Starting off to get into ketosis, daily net carb intake (total carbs minus fiber) should be less than 50g, ideally 20-30g, then increased slowly until an optimal carb intake is reached. This may be different for individuals. Most people stay in ketosis at around 20-30 net carbs daily. You aim to find the carb limit that allows you to stay in ketosis.

3. The daily proportion of calories that come from healthy fats should be increased.

4. Protein consumption should be moderate. The best way to figure out this is to use your body fat percentage to get an evaluation of how much protein you should be consuming.

5. If you've set your net carb limit very low (for weight loss or therapeutic reasons) at 20g a day and below, fruit and low-carb treats are best avoided.

6. Sodium, potassium, and magnesium may become deficient during ketosis, so consulting with a nutritional therapist is advised during a transition into a keto diet. Himalayan salt or Sea salt should be used in cooking.

7. You'll learn to eat when you are hungry, not because the clock (or anyone else) tells you to.

8. You'll stop eating when you feel full as the keto diet has a natural appetite control effect, so you will begin to eat less.

9. It's important to stay hydrated, being mindful of your water intake. Ideally drinking about 2l water daily.

10. Starting out, it's crucial to monitor your carb, fat and protein intake to get into ketosis and so that you don't kick yourself out of ketosis once in. Macro counting apps or specific keto apps that log your daily intakes are recommended.

What Are Ketogenic Fat Bombs?

Ketogenic fat bombs are small snacks or treat that is high in fat and low in carbs that you can eat as a quick breakfast, as a quick mid-afternoon snack, as a pre- or after- workout snack, or as extra fuel during your day.

A few facts about ketogenic fat bombs to help you understand them better:

1. Ketogenic fat bombs are often small

It's tough to overeat of these, so they take the shape of small balls or mini muffins.

2. Fat bombs can be sweet or savory

The most of the fat bomb recipes are usually sweetened with sweeteners like stevia. This is because stevia is a low calorie (and zero-carb) sweetener that also doesn't cause stomach problems for people, unlike many sugar alcohols that are used in low-carb treats. If, however, you dislike using stevia, then feel free to use your low-carb sweetener of choice when making sweet keto fat bombs.

3. Fat bombs contain lots of healthy fats

Most ketogenic fat bombs contain coconut butter or coconut oil as an ingredient. Coconut oil thickens when refrigerated through making these fat bombs much more easy to eat.

4. Store your fat bombs in the refrigerator

Fat bombs include lots of fat, which is often liquid at room temperature, so make sure to keep these delicious treats in the fridge when you're not eating them. They'll usually last 1-2 weeks in the refrigerator in an airtight container. You can also freeze them. Do not forget to thaw them a bit before eating ☐

5. Fat bombs often also contain seeds and nuts

We suggest you try not to eat too many seeds and nuts on a ketogenic diet since the fats in seeds and nuts can become easily oxidized if the recipe requires them to be heated and some seeds and nuts are high in carbs (check out our table of carb content for nuts and seeds at the end). Just a quick note about peanuts. Peanuts are not nuts, it's a legume, so almond butter is used instead of peanut butter in ketogenic recipes.

How To Make Ketogenic Fat Bombs in 3 Easy Steps

STEP 1:

Mix all the ingredients in a mixing bowl or blender or food processor.

STEP 2:

Form small balls or else pour the mixture into muffin cups.

STEP 3:

Freeze or refrigerate for several hours until the mixture is solid.

Ketogenic fat bombs are remarkably easy to do – and if you follow these steps, you can make these amazing treats in no time.

Ingredients that go into ketogenic fat bombs.

There are 3 basic ingredients of every fat bomb recipe:

1. Healthy Fats

For Example:

coconut butter, almond butter, cocoa butter, coconut milk, coconut oil, , coconut cream (solid part of a refrigerated can of coconut milk), butter (ok if you're not sensitive to dairy), ghee (mostly lactose and casein free, especially if you get cultured ghee, so it doesn't present the same problems as other dairy products), avocado oil bacon fat

2. Flavoring

For Example:

sugar-free vanilla extract, 100% dark chocolate, cocoa powder, peppermint extract, spices, salt

3. Texture

For Example:

almonds, walnuts, cacao nibs, pecans, chia seeds, shredded coconut,

bacon bits (choose sugar-free)

Sweet Fat Bombs

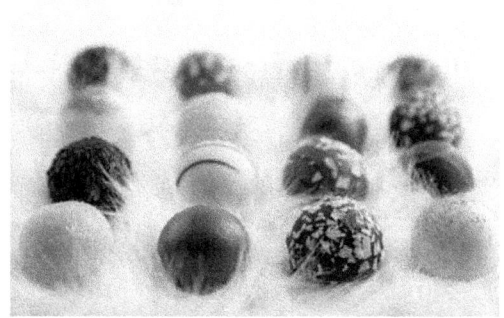

Vanilla Turmeric Anti-Inflammatory Keto Fat Bombs
- Prep Time: 20 minutes
- Serves: 5 fat bombs

Ingredients:

- 1/4 cup unsweetened coconut flakes and extra to garnish
- 1 Vanilla Shortbread Collagen Protein Bar
- 1/4 teaspoon ground turmeric
- 1/4 teaspoon ground ginger

- 1 tablespoon Lemon FATwater, or filtered water

Instructions:
1. Put the dry ingredients into a food processor. Blend until well mixed and crumbled.
2. Add the water to the food processor. Mix until dough forms.
3. Make five small balls out of the dough.
4. Roll the fat balls into more unsweetened coconut flakes.

nutrition facts
Serves 5
Serving Size: 1 Fat Bomb
Calories Per Serving: 62

Total Fat *5g*	Sugars *1g*	Cholesterol *0g*
Saturated Fat *1g*	Net Carbs *1g*	Sodium *26mg*
Total Carbohydrate *3g*	Dietary Fiber *2g*	Protein *3g*

Strawberry Fat Bombs
- Serves: 12 pieces

Ingredients:
- 1 cup sliced strawberries
- 2 tablespoons honey
- 1 teaspoon pure vanilla extract
- 6 ounces cream cheese, at room temperature

- 4 tablespoons unsalted butter, at room temperature

Instructions:

1. In the food processor, mix the vanilla, strawberries, and honey until relatively smooth.

2. Add the butter and cream cheese; and mix until smooth.

3. Scoop the mixture into muffin cups or ice-cube trays. Freeze until firm, at least 2 hours.

nutrition facts
Calories: 99

% DAILY VALUE

Total Fat *9g*	14%	Protein *1g*	2%
Total Carbohydrate *5g*	2%	Sugar *1g*	

Lemon Coconut Energy Balls

Serves: 4

Ingredients:

- 2 Lemon Cookie Collagen Bars
- 1/2 tbsp. raw honey, room temperature
- 1/2 tbsp. Brain Octane Oil
- 1/4 cup shredded organic unsweetened coconut
- 1 tbsp. lemon zest (optional)

Instructions:

1. Take a food processor or a fork and finely crush the bars.
2. Add in the honey and Brain Octane, blend into a mixture.
3. Fold in the crushed coconut and distribute evenly with a spatula or spoon.
4. Using a spoon to scoop, form each bite into the shape and size of a ping-pong ball. Sprinkle a little coconut and lemon zest (if desired) on the top to finish.
5. Refrigerate for one hour before serving.
6. Makes four lemon coconut energy bites, lasts up to 3 days if continuously refrigerated in a sealed container.

Lemon Bar Fat Bombs

- Total Time: 1 hour
- Prep Time: 10 minutes
- Serves: 30 fat bombs

Ingredients:

- 1 cup coconut oil, melted
- 2 cups raw cashews, boiled for 12 minutes or soaked for 2 hours
- Zest of 1 large lemon
- 1/2 cup coconut butter
- Juice of 2 large lemons
- 1/4 cup coconut flour
- 1/3 cup shredded coconut
- 1/16 tsp pink Himalayan salt
- 1/16-1/8 tsp powdered stevia (depending on your sweetness preference)

Instructions:

1. Add all the ingredients in the bowl of a food processor and mix until well-combined.
2. Move mixture to a medium-sized bowl and put in the freezer for 20-30 minutes to cool (they may take longer if you chose to boil the cashews rather than soak).
3. Remove mixture from freezer and form into balls.
4. Put balls in the freezer for 20 minutes to harden. I recommend putting them on a cookie sheet or plate lined with parchment paper to avoid the bottoms sticking.
5. Transfer from freezer once solid.
6. Enjoy!
7. Store in an airtight container in the fridge or freezer.

nutrition facts
Serves 30
Serving Size: 1 Fat Bomb
Calories Per Serving: 165

% DAILY VALUE

Total Fat *15g*	23%	Sodium *8.1mg*	0%
Total Carbohydrate *5.7g*	2%	Dietary Fiber *1.4g*	5%
Sugars *1.4g*		Protein *2.3g*	5%
Vitamin A *0µg*	0%	Vitamin C *6.3mg*	11%
Calcium *4.7mg*	0%	Iron *0.9mg*	5%

Fudge Fat Bombs

- Total Time: 2 hours
- Prep Time: 30 minutes
- Serves: 30 fat bombs

Ingredients:

- 1 cup coconut oil, at room temperature
- 1 cup almond butter
- 1 cup coconut oil, at room temperature
- 1/2 cup unsweetened cocoa powder
- 1/4 tsp powdered stevia OR 1-2 tbsp monk fruit sweetener, depending on sweetness preference
- 1/3 cup coconut flour

- 1/16 tsp pink Himalayan salt

Instructions:

1. On a medium heat in a small saucepan, melt and combine coconut oil and almond butter.
2. In the same pan, add dried ingredients and stir until well-combined.
3. Let mixture to cool slightly. Add additional sweetener if needed.
4. Pour mixture into silicone mold and place in freezer for 90 minutes OR pour into bowl (if you choose a silicone mold, skip steps #4 and #5 and allow the fat bombs to solidify in a freezer, about 3-4 hours).
5. Once solidified transfer bowl from freezer and form into balls.
6. Place formed balls on a plate or flat tray and return to freezer for 15-20 minutes.
7. Enjoy!

NOTES

Store fat bombs in an airtight container in the freezer. When you want one, pop one out, allow to thaw for a few minutes, and eat up!

nutrition facts
Serves 30
Serving Size: 1 Fat Bomb
Calories Per Serving: 128

% DAILY VALUE

| Total Fat *12.6g* | 19% | Dietary Fiber *2g* | 8% |

Total Carbohydrate *3.4g*　　1%　　Protein *2g*　　4%

Strawbwrries & Cream Fat Bombs

- Total Time: 1 hour
- Prep Time: 5 minutes
- Serves: 15 fat bombs

Ingredients:

- 1/2 cup coconut oil
- 2 cups frozen strawberries
- 1 cup raw cashews, boiled for 12 minutes or soaked for 2 hours
- 1/2 cup coconut butter
- 1/8 tsp – 1/4 tsp powdered stevia (depending on your sweetness preference)

Instructions:

1. In a microwave-safe bowl, microwave frozen strawberries until just thawed, about 45 seconds, depending on wattage strength of microwave.
2. Add all ingredients in the bowl of a food processor and mix until well-combined.
3. Transfer mixture to medium-sized bowl and place in freezer for 20-30 minutes to cool (they may take slightly longer to cool if you chose to boil the cashews rather than soak).
4. Remove mixture from freezer and form into balls.
5. Put balls in the freezer for 25 minutes to harden. I recommend putting them on a cookie sheet or plate lined with parchment paper to avoid the bottoms sticking.
6. Remove from freezer once firm.
7. Enjoy!
8. Store in airtight container in the freezer (allow to thaw before eating).

nutrition facts
Serves 15
Serving Size: 1 Fat Bomb
Calories Per Serving: 190

% DAILY VALUE

Total Fat *18g*	28%	Sodium *4.3mg*	0%
Total Carbohydrate *7g*	2%	Dietary Fiber *2.1g*	8%
Sugars *2g*		Protein *2.4g*	5%
Vitamin A *0.4μg*	0%	Vitamin C *8.2mg*	14%
Calcium *6.9mg*	1%	Iron *1.1mg*	6%

PBJ Fat Bombs

- Total Time: 1 hour
- Prep Time: 5 minutes
- Serves: 24 fat bombs

Ingredients:

- 2 cups frozen raspberries

- 3/4 cup peanut butter

- 1 tbsp melted coconut oil or Brain Octane or MCT oil

- 1/4 cup coconut oil

- 1/4 cup coconut flour

- 1/8 tsp – 1/4 tsp powdered stevia (depending on your sweetness preference)

Materials

- Ninja Professional Blender
- Silicone mold

Instructions:

1. In a microwave-safe bowl, microwave frozen raspberries until just thawed, about 1 minute, depending on wattage strength of microwave.
2. Add all ingredients in the bowl of a food processor and blend until well-combined.
3. Spoon mixture into a silicone mold and freeze for 1 hour.
4. Remove from freezer, pop fat bombs out of molds, and enjoy!

NOTES

Store in airtight container in freezer.

nutrition facts

Serves 24
Serving Size: 1 Fat Bomb
Calories Per Serving: 86

% DAILY VALUE

Total Fat *7.3g*	11%	Sodium *2.6mg*	0%
Total Carbohydrate 3.8*g*	1%	Dietary Fiber *1.9g*	8%
Sugars *1.1g*		Protein *2.3g*	5%
Potassium *17.6mg*	1%	Riboflavin (B2) *0mg*	1%
Magnesium *17.6mg*	4%	Iron *0.4mg*	2%

Pumpkin Spice Fat Bombs

- Total Time: 4 hours
- Prep Time: 10 minutes
- Serves: 24 fat bombs

Ingredients:

- 1/2 cup pecans

- Avocado oil cooking spray

- 1/2 cup pumpkin puree

- 1/2 cup coconut oil

- 4 ounces cream cheese, softened

- 1/4 cup golden monk fruit sweetener

- 1/4 tsp cinnamon

- 2 tsp pumpkin pie spice

Materials

- Silicone mold
- Electric hand mixer

Instructions:

1. Over medium heat in a small pot, spray avocado oil and toast pecans until fragrant. Remove from heat and set aside to cool.
2. In a small or medium-sized saucepan over low heat, melt cream cheese and coconut oil until combined.
3. Place the mixture into a medium-sized bowl and add pumpkin puree, monk fruit sweetener, and pumpkin pie spice. Mix using an electric hand mixer.
4. Scoop mixture into the silicone mold, top with toasted pecans, and sprinkle with cinnamon.
5. Place silicone mold in a freezer and freeze until solid, about 4 hours.
6. Pop fat bombs out of silicone mold and enjoy!

nutrition facts
Serves 24
Serving Size: 1 Fat Bomb
Calories Per Serving: 78

% DAILY VALUE

Total Fat *8.2g*	13%	Dietary Fiber *2.4g*	9%
Total Carbohydrate *3.1g*	1%	Protein *0.7g*	1%

Berries& Cream Fat Bombs

- Total Time: 4 hours
- Prep Time: 5 minutes
- Serves: 24 fat bombs

Ingredients:

- 2 cups frozen mixed berries

- 6 tbsp butter, softened

- 8 oz. cream cheese, softened

- 2 tbsp golden monk fruit sweetener
- 1 tsp vanilla extract

Materials

- Silicone mold
- Ninja Professional Blender

Instructions:

1. In a microwave-safe bowl, microwave frozen berries until just melted, about 1 minute, depending on wattage strength of microwave.
2. Add all ingredients in the bowl of a food processor and blend until well-combined.
3. Spoon mixture into a silicone mold and freeze for 4 hours, preferably overnight.
4. Remove from freezer, pop fat bombs out of molds, and enjoy!

NOTES

Store in airtight container in the freezer.

nutrition facts
Serves 24
Serving Size: 1 Fat Bomb
Calories Per Serving: 61

% DAILY VALUE

| Total Fat *5.9g* | 9% | Sodium *32.1mg* | 1% |

Total Carbohydrate 2.9g	1%	Dietary Fiber *1.5g*	6%
Vitamin C *3.5mg*	6%	Protein *0.8g*	2%
Calcium *9.2mg*	1%	Vitamin A *66.8μg*	4%

Dark Chocolate Peppermint Patty Fat Bombs

- Total Time: 1 hour 30 minutes
- Prep Time: 10 minutes
- Serves: 24 fat bombs

Ingredients:

Inner layer:

- ½ cup coconut oil, solid, room temperature
- 2 tsp peppermint extract
- ¼ cup heavy cream
- 3 tbsp shredded coconut
- 2 tbsp monk fruit sweetener or erythritol

Chocolate layer:

- 2 tbsp butter
- 2 tbsp + 1 tsp unsweetened cocoa powder
- 100g raw cocoa butter
- 1 tbsp heavy cream

Materials

- Silicone mold

- Hand mixer

Instructions:

1. Using a hand mixer, mix coconut oil, peppermint extract, monk fruit sweetener (or erythritol) shredded coconut, at high speed to turn the mixture into a paste.
2. Scoop mixture into a silicone mold. Put silicone mold in the freezer and freeze until firm, about 1-2 hours.
3. In a microwave-safe bowl, in 30- second increments, microwave chocolate ingredients until thawed, a little over 1 minute total (**see note below!). Mix after each microwave session. (The mixture should remain thick like melted chocolate).
4. Transfer silicone mold from freezer and pop coconut mixtures out.
5. Using a fork, carefully drabble coconut mixture into melted chocolate, put on parchment paper, and let harden in the freezer. (Optional: after ten minutes in the freezer, remove fat bombs and drizzle remaining chocolate over the top.)
6. When chocolate-coating has hardened, transfer from the freezer.
7. Enjoy!

NOTES

Store in freezer and allow to thaw and soften for about 10 minutes before eating.

**The microwave used in this recipe and melt the chocolate was 900 watts. If your microwave is stronger, you will need to decrease it to 50% power. If your microwave is much stronger than 900 watts melt the chocolate ingredients over a double-boiler.

nutrition facts

Serves 24
Serving Size: 1 Fat Bomb
Calories Per Serving: 104

% DAILY VALUE

Total Fat *11.7g*	18%	Sodium *1.5mg*	0%
Total Carbohydrate *1.6g*	1%	Dietary Fiber *1.3g*	5%
Iron *0.1mg*	0%	Protein *0.2g*	0%
Calcium *1mg*	0%	Vitamin A *20.6µg*	1%
Sugars *0.1g*			

Chocolate Chip Cookie Dough Fat Bombs

- Total Time: 1 hour 30 minutes
- Prep Time: 10 minutes
- Serves: 24 fat bombs

Ingredients:

- 1 stick unsalted butter, softened

- 8 ounces cream cheese, softened

- 1/2 cup crunchy almond butter

- 2 ounces 100% cacao Baker's chocolate bar

- 1/2 cup golden monk fruit sweetener

Optional Materials

- Silicone mold

Instructions:

1. In a mixing bowl of electric mixer, mix all ingredients except chocolate until well-combined.
2. Place mixture to a fridge for 30 minutes.
3. In a food processor, blend chocolate until broken into small pieces.
4. Remove mixing bowl from fridge, fold in chocolate pieces, and scoop and flatten into silicone mold or form mixture into balls. (If forming fat bombs into balls, line plate with parchment paper)
5. Harden fat bombs in a freezer for about 45 minutes.
6. Enjoy!

NOTES

Store fat bombs in an airtight container in the freezer.

nutrition facts
Serves 24
Serving Size: 1 Fat Bomb
Calories Per Serving: 98

% DAILY VALUE

| Total Fat *9.8g* | 15% | Sodium *32.2mg* | 1% |

Total

Carbohydrate 6g	2%	Dietary Fiber 4.8g	19%
Iron 0.3mg	1%	Protein 2g	4%
Calcium 21.1mg	2%	Vitamin A 72.2µg	5%
Sugars 0.8g		Magnesium 13.4mg	3%

Cinnamon Roll Fat Bombs

- Total Time: 1 hour 30 minutes
- Prep Time: 15 minutes
- Serves: 24 fat bombs

Ingredients:

Fat Bomb

- 8 ounces cream cheese, softened
- 1/2 cup butter, softened
- 1/2 cup crunchy almond butter
- 1/2 cup golden monk fruit sweetener
- 1 tsp vanilla extract
- 2 tsp cinnamon

Frosting

- 1 tbsp heavy whipping cream
- 1 1/2 ounces cream cheese, softened
- 1/4 tsp vanilla extract
- 2 tsp golden monk fruit sweetener

Instructions:

1. In a mixing bowl of electric mixer, mix all fat bomb ingredients until well-combined.
2. Place mixture to a fridge for 30 minutes.
3. Line plate with parchment paper.
4. Form mixture into balls and set fat bombs on a parchment-lined plate.
5. Harden fat bombs in the freezer for 45 minutes.
6. For frosting, using an electric mixer, mix all ingredients until fully combined.
7. Enjoy!

nutrition facts
Serves 24
Serving Size: 1 Fat Bomb
Calories Per Serving: 103

% DAILY VALUE

Total Fat *10.3g*	16%	Sodium *38.4mg*	2%
Total Carbohydrate *6.5g*	2%	Dietary Fiber *5.1g*	20%
Protein *2g*	4%		

Chocolate Chip Almond Butter Fat Bombs Bars

- Total Time: 2 hours 15 minutes
- Prep Time: 15 minutes
- Serves: 20 bars

Ingredients:

- 1 1/4 cup almond flour
- 3/4 cup almond butter, room temperature
- 1/3 cup golden monk fruit sweetener
- 1/2 cup and 2 tbsp coconut oil, solid, room temperature
- 1 tsp pure vanilla extract
- 1/2 cup chocolate chips

Instructions:

1. Line 8×8 baking pan with a wax paper or parchment.
2. To a medium microwave-safe bowl, add almond butter and microwave until soft, about 15-20 seconds.
3. To a bowl of softened almond butter, add almond flour, coconut oil, monk fruit sweetener, and vanilla extract. Take an electric mixer and mix all ingredients until well-incorporated. (If the almond butter or coconut oil is not incorporating well, place the bowl in a microwave for 10-15 seconds to soften the mixture.)
4. To the mixture, gently fold in chocolate chips until fully incorporated.
5. To a baking pan, pour in mixture and spread until mixture sits in an even layer.
6. Place to refrigerator for 2 hours.
7. Cut bars into desired size, and enjoy!

NOTES

Store bars in airtight container in the fridge.

nutrition facts
Serves 20
Calories Per Serving: 193

% DAILY VALUE

Total Fat *18g*	28%	Protein *4.2g*	8%
Total Carbohydrate *8.2g*	3%	Dietary Fiber *5.8g*	23%

French Toast Fat Bombs

- Total Time: 1 hour 25 minutes
- Prep Time: 10 minutes
- Serves: 24 fat bombs

Ingredients:

- 8 ounces cream cheese, softened

- 1 stick unsalted butter, softened

- 1/3 cup golden monk fruit sweetener

- 1/3 cup Maple-Flavored Syrup

- 1/2 cup almond butter

- 1 tsp maple extract

- 1/2 tsp pure vanilla extract

Optional Materials

- Silicone mold

Instructions:

1. In a mixing bowl, using an electric mixer, mix all ingredients until well-combined.
2. Freeze mixture for 30 minutes.
3. Remove mixing bowl from freezer and scoop and flatten into silicone mold or form mixture into balls. (If forming fat bombs into balls, line plate with parchment paper and set fat bombs atop parchment paper.)
4. Place fat bombs in a freezer for 45 minutes.
5. Enjoy!

nutrition facts
Serves 24
Calories Per Serving: 100

% DAILY VALUE

Total Fat *9.5g*	15%	Protein *1.9g*	4%
Total Carbohydrate *6.9g*	2%	Dietary Fiber *5.9g*	24%

Sea Salt Dark Chocolate Almond Cluster Fat Bombs
- Total Time: 30 minutes
- Prep Time: 10 minutes

Ingredients:

- 1 1/4 cup raw almonds
- 100g cocoa butter
- 5 tbsp unsweetened cocoa powder
- 5 tbsp heavy whipping cream
- Coarse sea salt
- 1/4 cup classic monk fruit sweetener

Instructions:

1. Preheat oven to 300F and line baking tray with parchment paper.
2. Bake almonds until toasted, about 10 minutes.
3. Line another baking sheet with parchment paper.
4. To a small glass bowl, add monk fruit sweetener, cocoa butter, cocoa powder, and heavy whipping cream.
5. Using double boiler method on a stovetop over low heat, melt ingredients together until chocolate is thaw. Mix mixture constantly to avoid burning.
6. Transfer melted chocolate from heat and stir in toasted almonds.
7. Spoon almond mixture and chocolate onto prepared baking sheet into desired cluster size. Top clusters with sea salt.
8. Place baking sheet to refrigerator and chill until firm, about 25-30 minutes. Alternatively, transfer baking sheet to freezer and chill until firm, about 10-15 minutes.
9. Once chocolate has hardened, gently pull parchment paper away away from clusters, serve, and enjoy!

NOTES

Store clusters in refrigerator or freezer.

nutrition facts
Serves 20
Calories Per Serving: 101

% DAILY VALUE

Total Fat *10.3g*	16%	Protein *1.9g*	4%
Total Carbohydrate *4.4g*	1%	Dietary Fiber *3.6g*	14%

4-Ingredient Keto Coconut Fat Bombs

- Total Time: 35 minutes
- CookTime: 25 minutes
- Prep Time: 10 minutes
- Serves: 38 fat bombs

Tools:

- Mini Ice Cube Tray
- Blender
- Saucepan

Ingredients

- ½ cup unsweetened coconut flakes

- 8 ounces coconut cream
- 1/3 cup coconut butter
- 1 tsp vanilla bean powder

Instructions

1. Bring the ingredients to a low simmer in a saucepan. Stir until smooth.
2. Transfer from the heat and cool for 2-3 minutes.
3. Transfer to a blender; blend on hight to remove any remaining lumps.
4. Place the mixture into a mini ice cube tray.
5. Freeze for 20 minutes or until set
6. Enjoy!

Ginger Fat Bombs

- Total Time: 5 minutes
- Prep Time: 5 minutes

Ingredients
- 2 ½ ounces coconut oil softened
- 2 ½ ounces coconut butter softened
- 1 tsp granulated sweetener of choice
- 1 ounce desiccated/shredded coconut unsweetened
- 1 tsp ginger powder

Instructions
1. Place all the ingredients in a pouring jug and mix until the sweetener is dissolved.

2. Pour into silicon molds or ice block trays and refrigerate for minimum 10 minutes.

nutrition facts
Calories: 120

% DAILY VALUE

Total Fat *12.8g*	20%	Protein *0.5g*	1%
Total Carbohydrate *2.2g*	1%	Dietary Fiber *1.4g*	6%
Sugars *0.1g*			

Keto Fat Bomb Pumpkin Pie Patties

- Total Time: 1 hour 20 minutes
- CookTime: 60 minutes
- Prep Time: 20 minutes
- Serves: 24 fat bombs

Ingredients

- ½ cup coconut oil
- 7 ounces unsweetened long shredded coconut
- 25 drops of alcohol-free stevia extract
- pinch to ¼ teaspoon Himalayan rock salt
- ¾ cup pumpkin puree, unsweetened

- 1 tablespoon ground cinnamon
- 1 ½ teaspoons ground ginger
- ¼ teaspoon alcohol-free pure vanilla extract
- pinch ground cloves
- ¼ cup grass-fed collagen, optional

Instructions

Line a baking tray with two 12-count mini muffin silicone molds.
1. Add coconut oil, shredded coconut, salt and stevia to the food processor. Pulse on high for 5-8 minutes until drippy.
2. Once smooth, remove ¼ cup of the coconut mixture from the food processor. Add remaining ingredients and pulse until smooth again. If you use cold pumpkin puree, the coconut will harden. No worries, process until smooth again.
3. Share the pumpkin mixture into the muffin cups. Press down with the back of a spoon or fingers until completely flat. Then, top with remaining white coconut mixture. Place baking sheet to the freezer and freeze for 1 hour.
4. Serve!

nutrition facts
Serves 24
Serving Size: 1 Fat Bomb
Calories Per Serving: 218
Calories from Fat 182

Total Fat *20.2g*   Sodium *38mg*
Saturated   Fat   Net Carbs *2.4g*
17.6g
Total
Carbohydrate *6g*   Dietary Fiber *3.6g*

Protein *3.6g* Sugars *1.9g*

Blackberry Coconut Fat Bombs

- Total Time: 10 minutes
- Prep Time: 20 minutes

Ingredients

- 1 cup coconut oil
- 1 cup coconut butter
- ½ tsp sweetLeaf stevia drops
- ½ cup fresh or frozen strawberries or blackberries or raspberries
- 1 tbsp lemon juice
- ¼ tsp vanilla powder or 1/2 tsp vanilla extract

Instructions

1. Place coconut oil, coconut butter, and berries (if frozen) in a pot and heat over medium heat until well combined. If using fresh berries, there is no need to cook them with the coconut oil and butter.
2. Add coconut oil mixture and remaining ingredients in a small blender or food processor. Blend until smooth. NOTE: Separation may take place if coconut oil mixture is too hot.
3. Spread out into a small container lined with parchment paper
4. Place in a fridge for one hour or until the mix has hardened.
5. Remove from container and cut into squares.
6. Store covered in the refrigerator.

Notes

To make coconut butter, place about 2 cups unsweetened dried coconut flakes into food processor and process until butter forms (about 7-8 minutes).

nutrition facts
Serves 16
Calories: 170

% DAILY VALUE

Total Fat *18.7g*	29%	Protein *1.1g*	2%
Total Carbohydrate *3g*	1%	Dietary Fiber *2.3g*	9%

Caramel Apple Pie Fat Bomb

Ingredients

- 2 medium green apples, cored and sliced
- 2 tbsp coconut oil
- 1 tsp cinnamon
- 1 can (5.4oz) coconut cream
- 1/2 cup coconut butter
- 20 drops English toffee stevia
- pinch sea salt

Instructions

1. In a saucepan, saute the apples in the coconut oils until soft.
2. Add the cinnamon and stir to coat.
3. In a high-powered blender, mix the rest of the ingredients and blend on high until liquefied.
4. Pour into silicone molds.
5. Place into the freezer until firm.
6. Pop out of molds and store in a plastic bag in the fridge.

nutrition facts
Calories: 86

% DAILY VALUE

Total Fat *8g*	14%	Protein *1g*	2%
Total Carbohydrate *3g*	1%		

Coconut Oil Fat Bombs

- Total Time: 20 minutes
- CookTime: 5 minutes
- Prep Time: 15 minutes
- Serves: 14 fat bombs

Tools

- Wax paper

- Blender
- Double boiler
- Baking sheet or plate

Ingredients

- 1/3 cup coconut oil, melted
- 2 cups shredded unsweetened coconut
- 4 ounces raw dark chocolate chips
- 2 tbsp raw honey
- ½ tsp vanilla bean powder, optional

Instructions

1. In a blender, add coconut oil, shredded coconut, vanilla bean powder and honey. Blend until mixture is fine and crumbled.
2. Line a plate or small baking sheet with wax paper. Using a tablespoon-size measuring spoon, scoop mixture and form into little mounds. Set onto parchment paper. Transfer to a freezer at 10 minutes to set.
3. Using a double boiler, thaw chocolate until smooth. Take a butter knife and drizzle coconut bombs with chocolate. Transfer back into the fridge to set 10 minutes. Store in refrigerator.

nutrition facts
Calories: 91

% DAILY VALUE

Total Fat *9g*	14%	Protein *1g*	2%
Total Carbohydrate *5g*	2%		

Creamy Coconut and Cinnamon Fat Bombs

- Total Time: 1 hour 30 minutes
- Prep Time: 30 minutes
- Serves: 10 fat bombs

Ingredients

- 8 floz coconut butter
- 8 floz coconut milk
- 1 tsp vanilla extract
- 1/2 tsp nutmeg
- 1/2 tsp cinnamon
- 1 tsp stevia powder
- 8 floz coconut shreds

Instructions

1. Take all the ingredients except the shredded coconut and place in the double boiler over medium heat.
2. While waiting for the ingredients to melt, mix them well.
3. Once all of the ingredients are combined remove the bowl from the heat.

4. Put the bowl in the fridge for about 30 minutes, until it is thick enough to roll into balls.
5. Roll the mixture into balls then cover them with the shredded coconut.
6. Refrigerate the balls for about 1 hour.

nutrition facts
Serves 10
Serving Size: 1 Fat Bomb
Calories Per Serving: 216
Calories from fat: 189

% DAILY VALUE

Total Fat *21g*	32%	Sodium *15mg*	1%
Saturated Fat *19g*	95%		
		Dietary Fiber *4g*	16%
Total Carbohydrate *8g*	3%	Potassium *70mg*	2%
Protein *2g*	4%	Vitamin C	0.1%
Iron	5%	Calcium	0.2%

Easy Vanilla Fat Bombs
- Total Time: 40-60 minutes
- Prep Time: 10 minutes
- Serves: 14 fat bombs

Ingredients

- ¼ cup virgin coconut oil
- 1 cup macadamia nuts, unsalted
- 2 tsp sugar-free vanilla extract or 1 vanilla bean
- Optional: 10-15 drops Stevia extract
- 2 tbsp healthy low-carb sweetener

Instructions

1. Place the macadamia nuts into the bowl of food processor and pulse until smooth.
2. Mix with softened butter and coconut oil (room temperature or melted in a water bath).
3. Add sweetener
4. Pour into mini muffin forms or an ice cube tray. You should be able to fill each one about 1 1/2 tablespoons of the mixture to get 14 servings. Refrigerate for at least 30 minutes and let it solidify.
5. When done, keep refrigerated. Coconut oil and butter get very soft at room temperature.
6. Enjoy!

nutrition facts
Serves 14
Serving Size: 1 Fat Bomb
Calories Per Serving: 132

% DAILY VALUE

| Total Fat *14g* | 20% | Sodium *15mg* | 1% |

Saturated Fat *7g*	35%			
		Dietary Fiber *4g*		16%
Total Carbohydrate *1.6g*	0%	Potassium *36mg*		2%
Protein *0.79g*	2%	Magnesium *13mg*		3%

Craving Buster Fat Bombs

- Total Time: 2 minutes
- Prep Time: 2 minutes
- Serves: 32 fat bombs

Ingredients

Single Serving:

- 1/2 Tbsp almond butter

- 1/2 Tbsp melted organic coconut oil

- 1/2 Tbsp organic cacao powder

Makes 32:

- 1 cup almond butter
- 1 cup melted organic coconut oil
- 1 cup organic cacao powder

Instructions

Single Serving Fast Method:

Melt the coconut oil, add the almond butter and cacao, and eat right away.

32 Servings Method:

1. Melt the coconut oil and stir in the almond butter and cacao until no lumps remain. Spoon 1/2 Tbsp of the mixture each into 32 small paper muffin cups.

2. Freeze or refrigerate until hard.

3. Enjoy!

NOTES

Store in the refrigerator.

nutrition facts
Serves 32
Serving Size: 1 Fat Bomb
Calories Per Serving: 122.5

% DAILY VALUE

Total Fat *11.75g*	18%	Sugar *0.5mg*	
Total Carbohydrate *2.25g*	1%	Protein *1.75g*	4%

Coconut Fat Bombs

Serves 30 fat bombs

Ingredients

- 6 ounces organic coconut oil
- 1-ounce cocoa butter
- 2 ounces organic coconut cream concentrate
- 3 tablespoons Honeyville blanched almond flour
- 3 tablespoons organic coconut flour
- 1 splash organic vanilla extract
- 1 pinch sea salt (real salt)
- 1 medium lemon, juiced & zested
- Liquid Stevia to taste
- ½ cups macadamia nuts
- ½ cup organic shredded coconut sweetened

Instructions

1. In a small pan, over low heat melt cocoa butter, coconut cream concentrate, and coconut oil.
2. In a blender, combine melted mixture with the lemon juice/zest, flours, vanilla, and stevia (adjust stevia to taste). Blend until well combined.
3. Add shredded macadamia nuts and coconut, pulse a few times to combine and lightly chop.
4. Press into a silicone mold or portion into bite-sized balls and freeze until firm.
5. Enjoy refrigerated or frozen.

Recipe Notes

Use 1 tablespoon of keto-friendly sweetener in place of stevia, if desired.

Peppermint Chocolate Fat Bombs

- Prep Time: 30 minutes
- Serves: 30 fat bombs

Ingredients

- 1/4 cup Cocoa Butter melted
- 1/4 cup Coconut Oil melted
- 1/2 cup Coconut Butter melted
- 1/4 cup MCT Oil
- 1 tsp Peppermint Extract
- 1/4 cup Collagen Protein
- 1/2 cup Cocoa Powder
- 3 scoops Prebiotin Prebiotic Fiber
- 1/4 tsp Monk Fruit
- 1/4 tsp Salt
- 1/2 cup Unsweetened Shredded Coconut

Instructions

1. Put chocolate molds of your choice on a flat surface that will fit in your freezer/fridge. Set aside.
2. Combine the coconut oil, melted cocoa butter, MCT oil, peppermint extract and coconut butter. Whisk to combine everything until smooth.
3. Add in the collagen, cocoa powder, prebiotic fiber, monk fruit, salt. Whisk to combine everything until smooth. Add in the unsweetened shredded coconut and mix to combine.
4. Transfer the chocolate mixture to a container with a pour spout (not required but makes pouring into the molds much more comfortable). Fill the molds entirely and put them in the freezer or fridge.
5. Remove fat bombs from the molds and store in an airtight container in the fridge for 1 month or the freezer for up to

6months. Let sit at room temperature for a few minutes before eating to allow them to soften a little

nutrition facts
Serving Size: 1 Fat Bomb
Calories Per Serving: 87
Calories from Fat: 72

% DAILY VALUE

Total Fat *8g*	12%	Total Carbohydrate *1g*	0%
Saturated Fat *6g*	30%	Dietary Fiber *1g*	4%
Sodium *21mg*	1%	Protein *2g*	4%
Potassium*30mg*	1%	Vitamin C	0.1%
Calcium	0.3%	Iron	1.8%

Raspberry Almond Chocolate Fat Bombs

- Prep Time: 5 minutes
- Total Time: 1 hour 5 minutes
- Chill Time: 1 hour

- Serves: 20 fat bombs

Ingredients

- 1/4 cup almond butter
- 1/2 cup coconut butter
- 1 tbsp unsweetened cocoa powder
- 1/4 tsp stevia powder
- 20 g raw almonds
- 20 g walnuts
- 1/4 cup raspberries frozen

Instructions
1. In a bowl, mix the coconut butter, almond butter, stevia powder and cocoa powder.
2. Chop the almonds and walnuts.
3. Microwave the raspberries for 40-60 seconds.
4. Put some parchment paper over a square pan and pour the chocolate butter inside. Sprinkle the nuts over and cover with the melted raspberries.
5. Place in the freezer for at least one hour. Take it out and break it into eight pieces (or more if you want smaller portions). Always keep frozen.

Recipe Notes

If your coconut butter is frozen due to the cold weather, microwave it before use until it's runny.

nutrition facts

Serving Size: 1 Fat Bomb
Calories Per Serving: 82
Calories from Fat: 65

% DAILY VALUE

Total Fat *7.26g*	11%	Total Carbohydrate *3.16g*	1%
Saturated Fat *0.55g*	3%	Dietary Fiber *1.7g*	7%
Sugars *0.86g*		Protein *3.09g*	6%

Keto Fat Bombs with Cacao and Cashew

- Prep Time: 15 minutes
- Total Time: 20 minutes
- Cook Time: 5 minutes
- Serves: 20 fat bombs

Ingredients

- 1 cup Coconut Oil
- 1 cup Almond Butter
- ¼ cup Coconut Flour
- ½ cup Cacao Powder
- 1 cup Raw Cashews

Instructions

1. In a non-stick medium pan over medium heat, heat coconut oil, and almond butter until mixed evenly, stirring often.
2. Pour the mixture from the pan into a bowl and mix in cocoa powder and coconut flour.
3. Set the bowl in the freezer for about 15 minutes until mixture cools and is stable.
4. While the mixture is chilling, place the cashews in a food processor and pulse lightly for a chopped texture.
5. When the coconut mixture is thickened, take 1/2 tablespoon of the mixture from the bowl, form into a ball, and dip in the blended cashews. Repeat until you have used all of the mixtures.
6. Refrigerate the fat bombs for 5 minutes.
7. Enjoy!
8. Store your leftover fat bombs in the refrigerator. Otherwise, they will melt quickly.

nutrition facts
Serving Size: 1 Fat Bomb
Calories Per Serving: 217

% DAILY VALUE

Total Fat *20.7g*	32%	Total Carbohydrate *6.6g*	2%
Saturated Fat *10.4g*		Dietary Fiber *2.1g*	8%
Sugars *0.9g*		Protein *4g*	8%

| Cholesterol 0mg | 0% | • Calcium | 5% |

Chocolate Almond Butter Collagen Fat Bombs

- Prep Time: 5 minutes
- Total Time: 25 minutes
- Cook Time: 20 minutes
- Serves: 30 fat bombs

Ingredients

- 1/4 cup coconut butter
- 1/4 cup coconut oil
- 3 tbsp cacao powder
- 1/2 cup almond butter
- 1/8 tsp sea salt
- 1 tsp vanilla extract
- Optional: sweetener of your choice
- 1/4 cup grass-fed collagen

Instructions
1. In a small saucepan, heat almond butter, coconut butter, and coconut oil, over low heat until melted.
2. Add the remaining ingredients and stir together.
3. Pour the mixture in a silicone form of your preference. Freeze for about 20 minutes until the fat bombs harden.

Store in the refrigerator or freezer.
4. If you don't have a silicone mold, you can pour the mixture in a small pan, freeze, then cut into bite-sized squares.

nutrition facts
Serving Size: 1 Fat Bomb
Calories Per Serving: 67
Calories from Fat: 54

% DAILY VALUE

Total Fat *6g*	9%	Total Carbohydrate *1g*	0%
Saturated Fat *3g*	15%	Dietary Fiber *1g*	4%
Polyunsaturated Fat *1g*		Sodium *38mg*	2%
Monounsaturated Fat *4g*		Potassium *73mg*	2%
Sugars *1g*		Protein *2g*	4%
Cholesterol *0mg*	0%	• Calcium	3%
		Iron	2%

Coconut Berry Fat Bombs

Ingredients

- 1/2 cup mixed frozen berries, such as cherries, strawberries raspberries, blueberries, pomegranates
- 1 cup refined coconut oil
- 1 teaspoon vanilla extract
- 14 drops SweetLeaf clear liquid stevia (or substitute honey to taste)

Instructions

1. Gently melt coconut oil on the stove. While the oil is melting, briefly process the frozen fruit in a food processor, so it's chopped up into small pieces.
2. Add the vanilla extract and stevia to your food processor.
3. Pour the melted coconut oil into your food processor and process to mix with the fruit and other ingredients. Continue processing until all of the fruit is smoothly blended into the oil.
4. The mixture should now be a thick blended consistency. If your mixture is still frozen and not mixing well, you can transfer some of the frozen pieces and melt them on your stove. Once melted, return the mixture to the food processor and try again to mix everything smoothly.
5. Scoop finished mixture into molds or drop spoonfuls on a parchment paper-lined surface such as a cutting board. Using the molds will make your coconut berry delights prettier, but

just dropping them as spoonfuls work just as well if you don't have or don't want to use molds.
6. Place parchment paper-lined surface or molds into the freezer to firm up the delights. After 30 minutes or so, or whenever they have become stable, remove from the molds/parchment paper.
7. Enjoy!
8. Store in a container in the freezer.
9.

nutrition facts
Serving Size: 1 Fat Bomb
Calories Per Serving: 96

% DAILY VALUE

Total Fat *11g*	17%	Net Carbohydrate *0g*	0%
Protein *0g*	0%		

Samoa Fudge Bombs

- Prep Time: 15 minutes
- Total Time: 15 minutes

Ingredients

Fudge Bomb:

- 2 ½ tbsp butter melted
- 3 ½ tbsp cocoa powder
- 3 ½ tbsp sweetener of choice

- 2 tbsp unsweetened coconut milk or heavy cream
- 2 ½ tbsp coconut oil melted

Caramel Coating:

- 2 ½ tbsp butter
- 2 ½ tbsp sweetener
- 2 tbsp heavy cream or full-fat coconut milk
- ⅛ tsp molasses, or low carb maple syrup, or yacon syrup
- ⅛ tsp vanilla extract

To Garnish:

- 1 tbsp unsweetened shredded coconut

Instructions

1. In a mixing bowl combine all the fudge bomb ingredients. Mix completely.
2. Pour or spoon mixture into a lightly greased mold, or ice cube tray, or a cake pop pan.
3. Freeze for 15 minutes or until firm.
4. In a saucepan over medium heat melt the 2 ½ tablespoons butter for the caramel coating.
5. Once melted add the 2 ½ tablespoons sweetener, 2 tbsp heavy cream or coconut milk and ⅛ teaspoon molasses, or low carb maple syrup. Mix and heat until bubbling. Transfer from heat and stir in ⅛ tsp vanilla extract. Let caramel sauce rest for a couple of minutes until it thickens a little.
6. Transfer fudge bombs from the freezer and place on a baking sheet lined with wax paper or parchment paper.
7. Drizzle or spoon caramel sauce over truffle bombs and sprinkle with shredded coconut.

8. Enjoy!
9. Store in covered container in freezer or fridge.

nutrition facts
Serving Size: 1 Fat Bomb
Calories Per Serving: 102
Calories from Fat:99

% DAILY VALUE

| Total Fat 11g | 17% | Total Carbohydrate 1g | 0% |

Keto Matcha Coconut Fat Balls

- Prep Time: 10 minutes
- Total Time: 1 hour 10 minutes
- Cook Time: 1 hour
- Serves: 16 fat bombs

Ingredients

- 1 cup organic coconut milk
- 1 cup organic coconut butter melted
- 4 tablespoons organic coconut oil melted
- 2 teaspoon organic vanilla extract
- 1 teaspoon organic ground cinnamon
- 4 tablespoon organic maple syrup
- 4 scoops Vital Proteins Matcha Collagen
- 1/2 cup organic shredded coconut
- 1/2 cup organic hemp seeds

Instructions

1. In a high-powered blender, add all ingredients. Blend until smooth.
2. Refrigerate mixture for about one hour until firm.
3. Using a small ice cream scoop, form the cold mixture into 32 little balls, roughly the size of a ping-pong ball.
4. Roll the balls quickly by hands to smooth them into round spheres, then drop each ball into the coconut/hemp seed mixture and roll them until thoroughly coated.

5. Enjoy!

Recipe Notes

To store, transfer your finished fat bombs to an airtight container and keep in the fridge for up to 2 weeks or in the freezer for up to 1 month.

**Note: The nutrition panel does not include 20 mg of L-Theanine, which is found in 2 scoops of the Matcha collagen. But there are myriad nutrients in green tea, including Vitamin C, B2, E and folic acid.

nutrition facts

Serving Size: 1 Fat Bomb

Calories Per Serving: 240

% DAILY VALUE

Total Fat 19.9g	31%	Total Carbohydrate 11.4g	4%
Sodium 37.7mg	2%		
		Dietary Fiber 2.4g	10%
		Sugars 7.9g	
Protein 6.4g	13%		
Cholesterol 0mg		Potassium	5%
Phosphorus	13%	Magnesium	14%
Thiamin (B1)	6%	Iron	7%
Riboflavin (B2)	6%		

Almond Pistachio Fat Bombs

Serves: 36 squares

Ingredients

- ½ cup cacao butter, finely chopped and melted
- 1 cup all natural roasted almond butter
- 1 cup creamy coconut butter
- 1 cup coconut oil, firm
- ½ cup full - fat coconut milk, chilled overnight
- ¼ cup ghee
- 1 tbsp pure vanilla extract
- 2 tsp chai spice
- ¼ tsp pure almond extract
- ¼ tsp Himalayan salt
- ¼ cup raw shelled pistachios, chopped

Instructions

1. Line a 9-inches square baking pan with parchment paper, leaving a little bit hanging on each side. Set aside.
2. Melt the cacao butter in a small pan set over low heat or in the microwave, often stirring.
3. Add all the ingredients, except for shelled pistachios and cacao butter to a large mixing bowl. Combine with a hand mixer, starting on low speed and progressively moving to high until all the ingredients are well combined, and the mixture becomes light and airy.

4. Pour the melted cacao butter right into the almond mixture and resume mixing on low speed until it's well combined.
5. Transfer to prepared pan spread as evenly as possible and sprinkle with chopped pistachios.
6. Refrigerate until entirely set, at least 4 hours but preferably overnight.
7. Cut into 36 squares and splurge!

Notes

*Note that it's fairly important that your coconut oil is firm so place it to the refrigerator for a little bit if you have to. Same goes for the coconut milk.

nutrition facts

Serving Size: 1 Fat Bomb

Calories Per Serving: 170

Calories from Fat: 157

% DAILY VALUE

Total Fat *17.4g*	27%	Total Carbohydrate *3.1g*	1%
Saturated Fat *11.1g*	56%	Dietary Fiber *1.5g*	6%
Sodium *18mg*	1%	Potassium	5%
		Iron	3%
Protein *2.2g*	2%		

Cholesterol 4mg	1%	Vitamin A	1%
Calcium	2%		

Almond Butter Maple Collagen Fat Bombs

- Time: 10 minutes
- Serves: 12-14 fat bombs

Ingredients

- 2 tbsp maple syrup, room temp
- ½ cup smooth, unsweetened almond butter, room temp
- ¼ cup pecans, finely chopped
- 2 tbsp coconut oil, melted
- 2 tbsp shredded coconut
- 2-3 scoops Further Foods Collagen Peptides
- 1 tbsp hemp seeds
- 1 tbsp Tin Star Brown Butter Ghee
- pinch of Redmond Real Salt
- 1 tsp black or brown sesame seeds
- additional chopped coconut and pecans for coating (optional)

Instructions

1. Mix everything (except for the extra pecans and coconut for coating) together in a food processor till well combined.
2. Transfer mixture out of food processor container into a bowl and refrigerate for about an hour to harden up a bit.

3. Remove from refrigeration and roll into balls. We use a two tsp ice cream scoop, or you can scoop out with a small spoon.
4. Roll completed balls in additional finely chopped pecans or shredded coconut. Place in refrigerator until ready to enjoy. You should get 12-15, depends on how large you want to roll them.
5. Store in fridge or freezer. Before freezing, place them all separately on a plate, once frozen they can then be placed in a bag for storing.

nutrition facts
Serving Size: 1 Fat Bomb
Calories Per Serving: 120

% DAILY VALUE

Total Fat *10g*	17%	Net Carbohydrate *3g*	1%
Protein *4g*	4%		

Coconut Carrot and Ginger Fat Bombs

- Prep Time: 10 minutes
- Total Time: 1 hour 10 minutes
- Cook Time: 1 hour
- Serves: 30 fat bombs

Ingredients

- ½ cup coconut oil solid
- ½ cup coconut butter
- ¼ cup chilled coconut milk
- ¼ cup chopped cashews
- 1 - 2 tablespoons cashew meal (optional)
- 2 carrots blend or grated until finely diced
- 2 heaping teaspoons ground ginger or a knob of freshly grated ginger
- 1 teaspoon ground cinnamon
- ⅛ tsp sea salt
- 1 teaspoon vanilla extract
- 2-3 tablespoons honey, maple, rice syrup or coconut nectar
- Shredded coconut for rolling

Instructions

1. Make sure your coconut oil is solid. Place it in the fridge for an hour or two if it is needed.
2. Place solid coconut oil and coconut butter into a bowl and whip with beaters or in a blender.

3. The mixture should become creamy and soft.
4. Add in chilled coconut milk and beat again.
5. Add in the rest of the ingredients and beat until well combined.
6. Taste and see if the flavors are right.
7. Place mixture in the fridge for up to an hour to harden.
8. The mixture should be the right consistency to roll.
9. Roll into small balls about two teaspoons per ball.
10. Roll in shredded coconut and place in a container or on a tray.
11. Pop into the fridge to set for about ½ an hour.
12. Eat and enjoy!

nutrition facts
Serving Size: 1 Fat Bomb
Calories Per Serving: 87

% DAILY VALUE

Total Fat *8g*	16%	Net Carbohydrate *3g*	1%
Protein *1g*	1%		

www.ingramcontent.com/pod-product-compliance
Lightning Source LLC
Chambersburg PA
CBHW071440070526
44578CB00001B/162